Lipstick

AND

DIPSTICK'S

*Essential Guide
to Lesbian Relationships*

by
GINA DAGGETT
and
KATHY BELGE

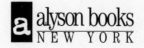

Manufactured in the United States of America

This trade paperback original is published by Alyson Books
245 West 17th Street, New York, NY 10011
Distribution in the United Kingdom by Turnaround Publisher Services Ltd.
Unit 3, Olympia Trading Estate, Coburg Road, Wood Green
London N22 6TZ England

First Edition: November 2007

07 08 09 10 11 **a** 10 9 8 7 6 5 4 3 2 1

ISBN: 1-59350-022-X
ISBN-13: 978-1-59350-022-1

Library of Congress Cataloging-in-Publication data are on file.

Cover photo by Maggie Parker
Interior design by Charles Annis

This book is dedicated first and foremost to Texas and Tiger, and then to all the women we've loved before them, whose dysfunctions, dry humping, and delicious dinners we reference in the following pages.

ACKNOWLEDGMENTS

We'd like to give a big shout out to Editor Shannon Berning—thank you for asking us to write this book—as well as to our friends at *Curve* magazine, with extra sugar to Executive Editor Diane Anderson-Minshall, Publisher Frances Stevens, Sara Jane Keskula, Catherine Plato, Danie Belfield, Malinda Lo, and all our faithful readers. We'd like to send love to the following peeps who continue to support and offer their savvy selves to our work and lives: Shea Steel, Tay Juncker, Mary Belge, Maggie Parker, Kelly Staley, Wade McCollum, Noah Jordan, Julianna Jaffe, Lucy Pascal, Stacy Bias, Shanna Germain, Jodi Helmer, Andrea Carlisle, Mary Foulk, Christine Calfas, Diane Benscoter, Beth Richman, Byron Beck, Shoshanah Oppenheim, Chris Hayes, Lara Mendicino, Caron Parker, Gina James, Amy Pedersen, Katrina Humbert, Anamarie Stockwell, Adjoa Robinson, Dionne Fox, Marc Acito, Floyd Sklaver, Theo Aalto, Co O'Neil, Erica Brown, Holly Grubbs, Ali Astro, Pat LaValley, Alison Jones, Sherwin Klass, Marc Savoia, Jim Radosta, Ashleigh Flynn, Ondine Kilker, Bill Daggett Jr., Bill and Jennifer Daggett, Nana Powell, Lanie Whittle-Daggett, Doyle Walls, Zeljka Carol Kekez, Jen Gagner, Tina Hoogs, Christina Scott, Scott Dillinger, Emily Nemesi, Beth Gaughn, Devida Chacon, Roland Arnold, Ryan and Katy Page, Gwen Throckmorton, Melanie Santarius, Dr. Chelsea Crum, Shannon Bradley, Tatum Wright, Retts Scauzillo, Deborah Wakefield, Jim McVittie, the fine folks at Walker Macy, Kim and the Egyptian Club, Lucy Brennan at Mint, POWER UP, It's My Pleasure, In Other Words Books, Crush bar, the dykes of Portland, Oregon, the Lesbianlife.about.com community, the Portland coffee shops where we wrote this book—Haven, Three Friends, Costello's, Jackman Joe, and Concordia—and all of those unnamed who've been supportive of our brainchild.

CONTENTS

Part III: Intimacy and Sex

Part IV: Taking It to the Next Level

PROLOGUE: READ THIS!

Beloved readers,

Welcome to our essential guide to lesbian relationships. It feels a bit odd to be writing you a letter: usually, you're the one holding the pen, pouring out details about the trouble you're having with your girlfriend, or pining about the beautiful woman you see on your way to work whom you're dying to talk to. We're here to say: We can help! You can have her, and you can keep her, if you heed the advice in this book.

With over thirty years of relationship experience, we come to you like an open book. Imagine that? Two open books within an open book. In the following pages, we promise to be honest with you, we promise to dish out our tough love strategies, while also being playful and tender. Wait, did we just say we'd be tender? OK, there's a lot more crass honesty than tenderness, but we do our best to soften the blows. And that's what you're hungry for anyway or you wouldn't have picked up this sassy lesbian tome.

As usual, we offer no apologies for any offense taken about our positions because we simply speak our truth. Take it or leave it, or shove it up your ass if you want. We don't care what you do with the book once you're done pilfering the pages, but maybe you'll pass it on to your friend who just can't get herself together.

If you don't know who we are, for shame: We're advice columnists in *Curve* magazine (the number one best-selling lesbian magazine in the nation) by day, and prolific writers by night, trying to make it in this godforsaken literary world. One of us is the butch, the other's the femme. You connect the dots.

Like our column in *Curve*, we're not responsible for what you do with our guidance. If, for example, you take Dipstick's advice about seeking revenge on your girlfriend's ex-girlfriend, don't call us to bail you out of jail, or come after us next. Likewise, if, by chance, the Water Dancer vibrator Lipstick suggests in the sex toy section gives you a little more than a tickle in the hot tub—like deep frying your titties—please don't sue us.

If you want your relationships to succeed, want to engage in healthy, fruitful communication, and want to have lots of sex, then kick off your shoes (your boots or your heels), relax, and listen up. You've come to the right place.

Yours truly,
Lipstick & Dipstick

PS: This book shouldn't be used as a flotation device, a hot pad at the lesbian potluck, or a doorstop. Read it, love it, and regurgitate it like it's the gospel. And be sure to brush up on your lesbian lingo in Lipstick & Dipstick's Gay Girl's Glossary at the end.

PART I

The Honeymoon

CHAPTER ONE

So, You've Met Someone

Y ou've been wishing for a girlfriend on every birthday candle, in every fountain, and on every shooting star since you were old enough to say cunnilingus . . . and now you've found her. Or so you think.

Lipstick & Dipstick are here to help you figure out if this dyke truly is the one for you and most importantly—when you discover that she is—how *not* to blow it.

How do you know she's it? Before you fly her home to meet the parents, before you take her last name, before you push that dolly holding your dresser into the U-Haul, listen to Lipstick & Dipstick.

Many lesbos never take the time to contemplate, they just dive into her panties and a new romance blindly. By the time the moving truck leaves and her cat is snuggling with your pussy, you're already convinced she's your solitary soul mate.

There are many factors that go into determining whether she's the "It Chick" or not. Here are a few questions to ask:

- Does she have a nice rack?
- Does she snore?
- Does she share your obsession with Sarah McLachlan?

Other things that are important include respect, communication, and love.

In this section, you'll get to take Lipstick's quiz to find out if your gal is the one, and you'll learn about jumping on trampolines, the

Lipstick's Quiz: Is She the One?

Take this quick quiz to find out if this girl is the one or not.

1. Your new flame's ex-girlfriend is:
    a. still her girlfriend.
    b. stalking her and has spit at you on more than one occasion.
    c. sleeping in the next room.
    d. sitting at the dinner table.
    e. now a man.
2. When you're on your way to her place, you:
    a. drop by your ex-girlfriend's to say hi.
    b. hit Dairy Queen for a Blizzard.
    c. break the speed limit.
    d. swing by a flower shop for a beautiful bouquet.
    e. are still at her house because you never left.
3. Your life before her was:
    a. wild, much more exciting than being pinned down.
    b. heterosexual.
    c. packed with one-nighters and lonely women.
    d. nothing compared to how it is with this fly bitch.
    e. can't remember what life was like before her.
4. When you go out to dinner, does she:
    a. talk only about herself.
    b. wait for you to pay.
    c. flirt with the waitress.
    d. chew with her mouth open.
    e. try to pick up the bill.
5. When you talk about politics, she:
    a. hands you a pamphlet about Exodus International.
    b. says that a woman will never be elected president.
    c. wants to talk about *American Idol*.
    d. is infuriated with the state of the union.
    e. tells you about the gay rights campaign she's working on.
6. On her living room shelves there are:
    a. no shelves, she's living on a friend's couch.
    b. no books at all.

     c. Fabio romance novels.

     d. nonfiction self-help books.

     e. pictures of her exes with their new partners.

7. When you play her a song you wrote, she:

     a. reads the newspaper headlines on the table.

     b. asks if you've written anything about her.

     c. wants to join in with her harmonica.

     d. asks where she can buy your CD.

     e. tells you you're beautiful and begs you to sing another.

8. When you're at her house for a nightcap, you:

     a. meet her girlfriend who's curled up on the sofa with the dog.

     b. can hardly get the door open because there's so much shit in the foyer.

     c. fall asleep to *Saturday Night Live*.

     d. struggle to find the right music because she has such great taste.

     e. take a hot bubble bath then feed each other truffles.

9. If her cell phone rings at dinner, she:

     a. sends a text message under the table while you're telling a story.

     b. after checking the screen, says she's sorry but needs to take the call.

     c. doesn't care and lets it ring.

     d. turns off her ringer immediately and apologizes.

     e. doesn't know because she's turned it off for the night.

10. Since you started dating, you have:

     a. wondered what it would be like back with your ex.

     b. dodged her phone call.

     c. written into Lipstick & Dipstick for advice.

     d. met her family.

     e. cried in her arms after sex.

You know the drill. Add up your points and see what Lipstick's crystal ball says.

a = 1 point

b = 2 points

c = 3 points

d = 4 points

e = 5 points

0–22 Points: Start looking for a new bathing suit . . . because you're headed to Dinah Shore in the spring to find a new love.

It's a good thing you came to Lipstick & Dipstick, as we'll be able to save you some time. This new girl ain't gonna cut it. You may still be hot and heavy in the sack, but there's no future. Enjoy it while it lasts—get in all the great sex you can—but don't go house hunting or ring shopping.

23–36 Points: Buy those tickets for that concert six months out . . . because you'll probably still be together.

Chances are pretty good you're gonna make it. Plan ahead, talk about living together, and take good care of your relationship. Especially in the beginning, it's important to nurture a new relationship so it continues to blossom for many years to come.

37–50 Points: Clean out your closet . . . because she's staying for good!

Girl, you're one of the lucky ones. This new lady is a keeper and you're very compatible. Have fun during the first few years of bliss, where you have nonstop sex and she can do no wrong. And then enjoy life as your relationship gets richer through the years.

importance of giving back to the world, and general things to keep in mind.

Don't be in such a hurry to tape that JUST MARRIED sign to your Subaru Outback or tattoo her name next to FOREVER on your panty line. Instead, with intuition and Lipstick & Dipstick as your guides, climb on-board and let's get this party started right.

Trampolines and Titillation

Getting off on the right foot

Lipstick: Have you ever been thrown off a trampoline?

DIPSTICK: Never. Have you?

Lipstick: Yes, and it fucking hurts.

DIPSTICK: You're nuts, Lip. Where could you possibly be going with this?

Lipstick: In the same way flying off a trampoline hurts like hell, every bone in your body feels like it's breaking when your relationship's falling apart. I've been in both places—the femme projectile and the heartbroken lover—so I should know.

DIPSTICK: You must've landed on your head.

Lipstick: Cute. My point is I didn't know what the hell I was doing on the trampoline back when I took that bad bounce, so I lost control and got injured. The same thing happens in relationships. Lesbians get in over their heads and start bouncing away, only to be puzzled when they wake up in the oleanders with a concussion.

So, we're here to help you jump properly and to teach you the ins and outs—and the ups and downs—of a successful lezbot relationship.

To start, here are ten things to keep in mind from the onset:

1. *Boogie*
   Dance like a motherfucker every chance you get! No matter where you are, don't ever refuse to dance; never cross your arms when people start filling the dance floor. Get your ass up and show the straight folk how the dykes do it.

DIPSTICK: I love dancing, Lip. You've seen me. But butches be careful. Remember when I kicked that girl in the face by accident?

Lipstick: I do. Even though you pulled a muscle and knocked that chick out, I've never seen someone jump so high off a speaker, and in a jackknife, to boot!

2. *Flirt*
   Always flirt with your girlfriend. I don't care if you've been together for twenty years, you should still be winking at her, pinching her ass, and saying suggestive things. Even if you're in wheelchairs, side by side in a nursing home—you reach for that damn bendable straw and lift up her muumuu with it. Forever keep that twinkle in your eye.

DIPSTICK: Pinch her rear? I'd get slapped for that.

Lipstick: Not me. My wife, Texas (a beautiful southern lass who's a fourth generation Texan), loves a good grab. Especially when she's wearing her assless chaps. Yee haw!

3. *Play*
   Let the good times roll. You know that friend who's so much fun to be around? They're the life of the party. Be that person and not only will your shininess rub off on those around you, but your relationship will be a blast.

DIPSTICK: If you don't know how to play, go see one. Can't dribble? Go to a WNBA game and cheer loudly. Can't sing? Who cares? Go see *Sing-a-Long-a Sound of Music* and sing off-key.

Lipstick: Yeah—get in the game whatever way you can!

4. *Laugh*
   Don't ever lose your sense of humor, especially when you and your girl-friend are having problems.

DIPSTICK: I've found the best way to end a fight is to crack a joke. One word of caution: it's usually better to have a laugh at your expense, not hers.

Lipstick: Good advice.

5. *Have sex*
   If it's summer, do it in the hammock; if it's winter, light a fire and shag on a furry rug.
6. *Listen up*
   Always listen to your girl, no matter if she's rambling nonsense.

DIPSTICK: Yeah, you've got to make sure you don't miss something important she's got to say. My wife, who I'll call T.I.G.E.R. (The Incredible Girl at the End of my Rainbow), likes to process. She's a product of the nineties and had way too much therapy, and Dipstick has a touch of attention deficit disorder, so when we've got something important to discuss, we get out of the house and walk. When we're moving, I have no problem paying attention.

Lipstick: Here are some tips for those who aren't so good at listening, whether stationary or on a nature walk:

- Shut your pie hole and let her speak.
- Look at her when she talks.
- Don't watch TV over her shoulder.
- Never mentally go over your to-do list when she's telling a story.
- Spend twice as much time listening as you do talking.

7. *Skydive*

Have you ever jumped out of a plane? If not, you should because it reminds you you're still alive. If not skydiving, do something else to get your blood pumping. A new relationship is a great place to start taking risks. Sit down with your new girlfriend and come up with a list of things you want to do before you die.

DIPSTICK: Machu Picchu and to see the Lady Volunteers in Knoxville are on my list.

Lipstick: Are the Lady Volunteers a group of women you do charity work with?

DIPSTICK: Basketball, ya freak.

Lipstick: Oh, riiiiight.

8. *Have sex*

When you're done with your list of things to do before you die, go have sex again. Take a bath this time—fill the tub with bubbles, line it with candles, and jump in! Then go to the bedroom and shut the windows so you can scream if your mood (or your girl) strikes you.

9. *Explore*

Don't be afraid to try new things (and I'm not only talking about in the bedroom). Push yourself every day and don't be afraid of anything. I mean nothing.

10. *Travel*

Have you always wondered what the sushi was like in Japan? Plan a trip. Texas and I travel all the time and, even after all these years, we still have more sex on the road than we do at home. Plan as many getaways as you can, and then be creative and spontaneous once you get there.

DIPSTICK: No matter if you've already flown off a trampoline, it's never too late to learn how to properly handle yourself. Beyond the above starter tips, there are all kinds of juicy nuggets coming up, so get yourself ready. For now, just remember to spot each other, take turns doing flips on your own, and NEVER be complacent, for it's the kiss of death.

Be Generous, Be Gracious

Give, give, give

Lipstick: I'm a lucky woman and I know it. I wake up every day full of gratitude and I try to harness this energy for the good of the world around me. By living with the intention, giving more than is expected, and devoting myself to family and Texas, I'm able to give something back to the universe. And this gift is important.

DIPSTICK: You're making yourself sound like Mother Teresa here. Is this the same Lipstick I saw cut some guy off at the post office yesterday?

Lipstick: I circled three times and that spot was mine. The universe put it there for me.

When it comes to your relationship, here are a handful of ways you can be generous:

With your time. Living in this fast-paced society, we struggle to balance work and our personal lives. Although you might want to go to judo seven nights a week, make time for your girlfriend, even if it means missing a match or two.

DIPSTICK: Pay special attention if she starts to moan that you're not around enough. At the end of your life, are you going to wish you made that last sales call or made love to your honey pie?

Lipstick:

With yourself. Open up about the intimate details of life: tell her about your fears, your past, about the time you peed your pants in grade school. Trust her and let yourself completely go in her presence. If you can't be yourself when you're with her, then where can you be authentic?

DIPSTICK: By "let yourself completely go" we don't mean not showering and wearing the same sweats for three weeks.

With attention. Be totally present when you're together. Give her your full attention. Leave everything else at the door.

Lipstick:

With gifts. Bring her small gifts, especially ones that are handmade, or a flower you picked on the way to her house. It's the little things that matter in a relationship.

DIPSTICK: So you're the one snipping hydrangea from my front yard! Never go broke for a girl, but pay attention. You'll win her forever when you buy that Easy-Bake Oven she wanted as a kid. I keep a list of ideas in my PDA and don't just wait for special occasions. The present is a perfect time for a present.

Lipstick:

With laughter. I can't stress enough the importance of laughter. A famous Yiddish proverb says, "What soap is to the body, laughter is to the soul." It's the truth. Remember to scrub-a-dub-dub.

DIPSTICK: Texas laughs at jokes like that?

Lipstick: Yep. She laughs because she loves me.

With affection. Hold her hand. Don't be afraid to steal a kiss in a restaurant if you feel compelled. This is a free world we live in, after all. Nuzzle her neck at a cocktail party and tell her something dirty, or something silly. Touch her and do it often.

DIPSTICK: Cool it when you're at dinner at her mom's.

With compliments. Tell her how beautiful she is, how amazing she looks. This is rarely a problem for me. Tiger looks hot in her workout clothes and her party duds.

Lipstick: That reminds me—I want to borrow the dress she had on Saturday night.

With love. Love her big and love her all the time. Don't hold back. We go through tough times personally, sure, but don't ever sacrifice what's most precious because you're having a difficult time. Always let her know you love her.

Give yourselves to the community

Open up your consciousness and look around you; opportunity is everywhere. Hearing the word *generosity* or *charity*, you might immediately think of money. That's a misconception. Your time and influence are just as valuable. Maybe the two of you could volunteer at a soup kitchen? Teach immigrants how to speak English? Mentor queer youth?

There's nothing more rewarding than giving time to your favorite charity, especially if it's an organization where you get hands-on experience with people. There's no better way to stay connected than by helping others. Give and give often.

Always be full of gratitude for what you have and each other.

CHAPTER TWO

Titties, Titles, and Testing the Water

S tarting a relationship is bliss, but it can also be challenging. They're sexually charged challenges, but nonetheless, you're just getting to know each other, so it's a constant learning curve. Like, what to do about accoutrement in the bedroom—do you buy new toys for the new girl? Is it OK to take off your clothes in a crowded club? And what about protection? Everyone knows what a dental dam is, but does anyone really use them? Perhaps most confusing: When do you go from friend to dating to girlfriend to partner? And what happens if you're on different pages? This section is all about the T's: titties, titles, and testing the waters.

Her Bra Is Still Stuck in the Fan

When you feel threatened

Sloan was known for her great tits. At Pride each year, there was always a strategic gaggle of girls lined up in the stands, jockeying for a good view of the parade and her cleavage. Even though those dykes tried to be inconspicuous behind their sunglasses, Sloan's girlfriend, Charlotte, was on to the vibe. She, after all, had been an ogler herself. She and Sloan had been in a monogamous relationship for two years and just closed on their first house together. Aside from her voluptuous bosom, Sloan was also known for her wild ways. The uninhibited soul, Sloan had, at more than one party, been the ringleader behind long games of strip poker. From a few feet away, as Charlotte sipped her martini, she watched Sloan shed her clothing piece by piece until everyone was either in her skivvies or skin.

This infuriated Charlotte and she'd talked to Sloan about it more than once. Despite her best effort, Sloan couldn't help herself and things reached a dangerous head when they were at the dyke bar one night. On the dance floor together, they were dancing the night away until Sloan, claiming she was overheated, decided to take her top off and launch her bra at the DJ booth, only to have it get caught on the ceiling fan. Rumor has it, it's still there today, spinning above the dance floor, slowly driving Charlotte insane while driving a wedge between her and Sloan.

Lipstick: Never, ever, ever take your bra off and throw it in a public establishment if the fans are on! Let's just hope it wasn't a new Infinity Edge bra from Victoria's Secret—they're pricey. It's hard to estimate how many bras have been lost in the smoky dive bar abyss, or after a one-night stand because you couldn't remember her name, or what her cross streets were.

DIPSTICK: I like to think the lady who left her bra at my house did so not because she lost my address, but so I'd have something to remember her by.

Lipstick: Dream on, Dip. If the above anecdote is ringing a bell, then you know what Circling Charlotte is dealing with—it's called I-don't-trust-my-girlfriend-and-I-don't-know-what-to-do syndrome.

Are you the one who feels totally alienated by your lover when she peels off her clothes and slides into a Jacuzzi full of lip-licking lesbians? Are you the one who loves your birthday suit? Either way, this situation is about more than getting naked. It's about boundaries, security, and comfort zones, and it must be dealt with or you can say good-bye to your long-term relationship (LTR).

As territorial beings, we have no choice but to, at times, feel threatened in our relationships. It's a knee-jerk reaction, something we don't always have control over. It could be something our lovers did, or it could be from some stupid dyke fresh out of the closet who's trying to snatch your girlfriend. (Seasoned dykes should know better.)

Regardless of the cause, the two of you must talk this out and establish some firm boundaries, ones that if crossed have repercussions (more than just a spanking). Shame on Sloan for not being more respectful of Charlotte's feelings and shame on Charlotte for letting this lacey pattern continue.

DIPSTICK: Hold up there little hussy. If I know Sloan—and trust me, I've met a few gals just like her—this is one wild child who won't be tamed. Nor should she! I know plenty of women who would be happy with Sloan's crazy ways. Wasn't it Sloan's licentious side that made Charlotte fall for her in the first place? Listen up ladies, if you're not happy with an exhibitionist partier, then let your little panther run free and find yourself a nice bunny rabbit.

Lipstick: No, Dipstick, I don't want to tame the lion, I just want to remind all the voluptuous vixens out there who like to drop trou about seven little letters that equal RESPECT, a very important word in lesbian relationship vocabulary. Has Charlotte talked to Sloan about this? Has she sat her down somewhere other than the club right after the tits-ident? If she's chosen to only address the issue in the dark corner of the bar, then this relationship is in trouble. Confronting a partner needs to be done in a private safe space (unless she's endangering her life or is about to cheat, then go ahead and make a scene). In an even-tempered, loving way, impart to your girlfriend that her behavior makes you uncomfortable and that you'd rather watch reruns of Bush's inaugural speech than go out drinking with her again. Leveling with your girlfriend will usually work. If it doesn't and she's still dancing on the tables without her over the shoulder boulder holder, then I say it's time to seriously consider if this is a woman you truly want to be with. If she says she's sorry, but she just got caught up in the moment, give her one more chance (we all deserve one more chance), but if the pattern continues, do you really want to be with someone who can't control her behavior?

That all said, I don't want you to get the wrong idea. All the work doesn't rest on Sloan's shoulders. You must ask yourself why her naked shenanigans get your panties in a twist. Perhaps you could use a shot of tequila or a hit from the bong.

But it's not so much about the nudity as it is that you don't trust Sloan, huh? Or you're too afraid to show your own boobies? And her uninhibited spirit makes you jealous. Nudity isn't a bad thing (unless you're at the dyke march stalled under a sappy tree, then it is—sap is hard to get out of pubic hair). Your insecurities may be hampering this relationship as much as her nudist colony membership. Sit down face-to-face with your clothes on and work it out. But you must remember, when dealing with each other, not only no bra flinging, but also no mud slinging!

DIPSTICK: Lipstick, why must you insist our sisters alter their conscious-nesses to lighten up? Boozing and doping don't solve any problems; they just mask them for a while. And most of the jealous types I know only get more so with each passing drink. Take it from Dipstick: you don't want to douse a girl like Sloan's flame. Instead, join her in the bra flinging. It will do you good to get out of those khakis and polo shirt anyway!

Your Bag of Old Tricks and Dicks

Sex toys from the past

Imagine this: So, you're good and horny and the moment has come for you and your new hot thing to knock the boots. There are candles, there is sexy music, and the mood is set. You're ready. Then your new girl reaches under the bed and pulls out a black leather harness and a red dildo. You're even more excited now and can hardly wait for her to get her hands on you. As she's fastening the buckles, she's giving you that loaded look. The big night is finally here! Then, as she's checking to make sure the harness is secure, she winks and unfortunately opens her mouth: "I've had this bad boy for years."

Boom! [Sound of inflatable raft losing its air.]

Immediately, you begin to run through a mental Rolodex of all those exes you've seen pictures of around the house. Molly from Miami, who had a pet iguana. Ruthie from Rochester, the dominatrix. And Bootsy from Beaver, Montana, who now lives on a lesbian commune somewhere in Wyoming. They all enter the room as your new love is getting the straps tightened up . . .

Lipstick: Just what you wanted to hear, right?

I suppose there are worse things that your new girlfriend could do or say, but there aren't many. Recycling your old sex toys—ones you've used with your ex and other lovers—is a definite homo no-no according to Lip-stick. It's a turnoff and it's grody to the max.

Out with vaginal voodoo

Vaginal voodoo: the juju that comes along with sex toys (or anything else) you've used or associate with other people, especially another partner.

After you go through a breakup, before you start dating again, first, get rid of the Indigo Girls CD you listened to nonstop when you were going through the "transition," and then, if you're ready, pitch all your former sexual accoutrements, save one or two you can use for a little you-on-you action. And lube is OK to keep, unless you're seeing someone who's super insecure. Use your best judgment there.

When you're going to have sex with your new girlfriend—one that you think is going to last—you'd best not use that old vibrator you and your ex buzzed into the ground. If you can afford it, pick up a new toy before you sleep with her. If it's a one-night stand, old sex toys are fine. Vaginal voodoo won't matter. If it's someone you really like, however, then be smart and keep your silicon sacred.

DIPSTICK: Lipstick, I disagree. For those of us trying to preserve the earth, reduce, reuse, and recycle is our motto. That's why our harnesses are not made of leather, but recycled bicycle tubes. Would you get rid of your bed, your sheets, and repaint your room every time a new lover came into your life? So why should you get rid of your sex toys?

Lipstick: Because you didn't shove the mattress—thank god—in your exgirlfriend's pussy.

DIPSTICK: Maybe a working-class butch had to scrimp and save for that red silicone pecker and she can't afford to dump it every time a girl dumps her. Instead, there four ways to handle the reused love handle with tact and class:

1. Never mention the last girl you shared your silver ding dong with. Don't even hint at it. Make love to her like it's the first time you've ever been with a woman. Well, maybe not like that—you do want to turn her on right?
2. Put a condom on that thing. This is important to prevent the spread of any diseases, but a condom is also a psychological barrier, keeping the past lover's energies from entering your new dame's psyche.

3. Some butches view their "toys" as an extension of themselves while having sex. You wouldn't suggest she get a tongue transplant or new fingers, would you? The dildo stays, too.

4. Let her know that this toy is for her and her only. Come on now, it doesn't take Don Juanita to know that no matter what accoutrements you use or don't use, you treat each and every new girl as if she were the only one special enough for you to take to this special place.

Romance her right and she won't be thinking about the toy between her legs, rather the hot woman handling it.

I Overheard Her Say We're Just Dating

When you're on different pages

Have you ever been on a different page than someone you're dating? We heard from a Seattle woman recently who was stuck in a quandary. Here's her sitch:

It was a Friday night and Sally and Helen were at a dinner party where they didn't know anyone but the hosts. During cocktail hour, they made the rounds meeting new people. As Sally talked with Tom, a stockbroker from the city, and ate a cracker loaded with goat cheese, she overhead Helen tell a nearby lesbian couple that Sally wasn't her girlfriend, they were just dating. They'd been together for two months and Sally thought differently, so all night, she fumed and pouted about what she'd overheard, mulling over how she could broach the subject without opening herself up to rejection. She never did find a way in, so she just let herself stew in the confusion and slowly began resenting Helen.

When does your relationship move from dating to girlfriends to partners? It's a fine line that, unfortunately, many women cross at different times.

DIPSTICK: The thing about lesbian relationships is that there are no hard and fast rules about when it moves from one stage to the next. You may be falling in love with your new girl, but she thinks you're just having fun. You may be dreaming of vacations in P-town and a getting a golden retriever while she's still planning to go to Gay Ski Week by herself and considers a goldfish too much responsibility.

How do you determine where your relationship is and where it's headed? Start by getting your head out of her hoo hoo. No one can think straight when all they see is pussy. And with your tongue free, it's time to start talking. Communication is the key to any relationship, but saying you love her too early may scare her off.

All relationships are different. Sometimes it's good to throw Tampax to the wind and jump right in with both breasts. Other times proceeding with caution makes more sense. What do you do when you and the one you're seeing don't match up?

First: Relax. Put it all in perspective. OK, so you found out something you didn't want to know, but knowing doesn't change anything. You probably feel like a fool, but at least now you understand why she didn't get you a gift for your two-week anniversary. It doesn't mean your relationship won't grow and change. In fact, it will. You can't control how another person feels, but you can change how you act and react. If you need to have a good scream or cry, go ahead. Just not at her. Once you've got it all out, then it's time to confront her.

Second: Talk to her about it. An unequal relationship is hard, no matter which side you're on. You can't force her feelings, and you can't change yours. Set aside a time to talk and let her know how you feel about her. See if she can tell you what's going on for her. If this is your first conflict, it can be telling about how you both will handle problems in the future.

Third: Reflect on what she said. When you talked, did she say, "Back off bitch, you're smothering me!" Or did she speak in "I" statements, telling you what's going on for her and why she's not ready to take the plunge into this relationship.

Fourth: Ask your friends. Maybe you're the type who falls fast for a new woman every three months. You're convinced she's the one and you'll never feel that way about someone ever again. Then you break up, and suddenly suffer from amnesia. You meet another hot woman and it starts all over again. Or maybe you've been single for so long and you've been wishing so hard for a relationship, that the first person who shows interest is IT, and you imagine yourselves in matching white chiffon walking down the aisle. What we often can't see about ourselves, our friends see in us, and if they're good friends, they'll keep their mouths shut about our little quirks. That is, until we ask. So ask.

Sit your closest friend down and get her opinion of the "relationship" you're entering. Value what she says. After all, she has your best interest in mind. Unless of course, she is secretly in love with you, then go to your best fag friend.

Fifth: You can't force her into something she's not ready for. Even if you are sure she's the one you've been dreaming about, visualizing, and saying affirmations about for the last decade, if she's not certain, you've got to accept that. This might be a good time to study Zen.

Lipstick: You're so pragmatic, Dipstick. You've got a five-step process for everything! Lipstick is more laid back and likes to go with the flow. Confront your new girl if you're feeling an imbalance, but be extra cautious if she's skittish and you think it might scare her off. It's true that lesbian relationships are typically on a fast track—we've earned the U-Haul jokes, after all—but that doesn't mean that's every lesbian's M.O.

I'd advise you to confront your new girl, but not to put unnecessary

---

Lipstick's Top Ten Signs It's *Not* Going to Work

1. She's already figuring out ways to help you spend your trust fund.
2. You've had to call the police on one of your dates.
3. You saw a Bush/Cheney sticker in her desk drawer.
4. Her boyfriend insists on Saturday nights.
5. She's a big Anne Heche fan.
6. She doesn't like you to spend time with your friends.
7. She's pissed you're reading this book because you guys don't need guidance.
8. She says she's "pretty sure" she's gay.
9. You overhear her tell her friends that she's stopped taking her meds and they're concerned.
10. Her girlfriend works at the Starbucks around the corner from your house, the one you like to hit on the way to work.

pressure on her because if she's anything like me, she'll be turned off by a beaver that's too eager. Use caution and play your cards well. If you want to be a successful gambler, don't show your hand too early.

DIPSTICK: Encouraging women to play games, Lipstick?

Lipstick: No, Dip. It was a metaphor, and a good one. Over-analyzing and over-processing a budding relationship can take a perfectly good thing and lace it in awkwardness, which, as we all know, typically leads to distance, which (without good communication) usually leads to the end.

If your heart is feeling more invested or if you want things to move faster than she does, take a step back, get some perspective, and relax. Quit focusing on the relationship and get yourself immersed in something else. Pick up your guitar again. Remember how you liked to run? How about training for your first marathon? Why not tackle that big house project you put on the back burner?

Keeping yourself occupied with something other than the status of your relationship will be a good thing; it will free up that energy you're spending dwelling on whether she did or did not call you and open up a world of possibilities.

No one likes desperation, and whining about it makes you seem just that, a desperate whiner. If you're feeling stress about the status of your growing relationship, chill out and let it unfold as it should. Don't be in such a hurry to slap labels on it. Enjoy each other's company, and focus on what's going right.

CHAPTER THREE

Friends, Ex-Lovers, and Enemies

You never know what your new girlfriend's sphere of influence is going to look like, but you can expect one thing: an ex-girlfriend or two. Is she the type that has lots of straight girlfriends, only one or two dykes, or is she a fag hag? Has she dated men or is she a gold star? Was she married? Did she have a baby? Is she an older dyke who's had more girlfriends than years you've been on the planet?

Regardless of whom your new girl surrounds herself with, there are likely to be joys and challenges. If you're lucky, you'll hit it off with most of these people. If you're not, then you'd better pay careful attention to the following sections. Do you feel the cold metal from the jealous friend's gun on your back? Have you woken up to the angry ex-husband pounding on the door? Does your new girlfriend still spend every holiday with her ex? Well, you're not alone. The "others" aren't going anywhere and neither are you.

When Did This Become a Crash Pad?

Dealing with her friends

Alyson first caught a glimpse of Mary on the rugby field. A friend with a crush on one of the players dragged her to a game. Alyson had never thought much of rugby, but once she saw Mary cut between two burly girls, causing them to crash into each other as she sprinted down the field for a goal, she was hooked. Later at the rugby party, Mary and Alyson exchanged numbers and soon they were sharing a bed. All was going great until late one night, on her way to the bathroom, Alyson tripped over a pair of cleats in the hallway. Turns out they belonged to Fierce, Mary's rugby buddy, who crashed at Mary's place from time to time. Fierce was not someone Alyson ever thought she would be friends with and here she was sitting across the breakfast table from her. Fierce complained of a hangover and bragged about the straight girl she'd bagged the night before. It took all of Alyson's strength not to say something rude. Every time Alyson saw Fierce she wanted to avoid her, but how could she? She was Mary's best friend, after all.

Lipstick: Let's face it: we can't get along with everyone. Normally, in our everyday lives, if someone bugs us, we can simply pull out the kitchen sheers and snip, successfully cutting the bad energy out of our lives. (It's important to eliminate negative impacts in your daily routine; vexatious spirits bring you down.) But what do you do when your new girlfriend's best friend drives you crazy? You can't exactly cut her out of your life, and if you try, you might cut off more than you hoped for. If your girl's friend—who we'll call Burr in your Butt (a.k.a. BB)—makes your heart rate spike there are several things you can do:

Strategy 1: Keep your distance. Steer clear of the bitch. Let your girlfriend hang out with BB all she wants, but conveniently be busy when they get together for happy hour. We know it's going to be tough to be separated for a few hours, but you can handle it and it's for you and your relationship's own good.

Strategy 2: Vent. Call up that friend you trust, the one who will listen for hours, and vent! And then vent some more. No need to be petty or cruel, but have your friend help you analyze why BB drives you crazy, so you can find the source of irritation. Maybe you can pull the burr out.

Strategy 3: Create a buffer. If that doesn't work, make that same friend you vented to come to any events where BB will be. Have her sit between you and the bugger. This will soften the thorns and help you keep your sanity.

Strategy 4: BYOB. When all else fails, make sure there's alcohol any time you're forced to hang out. Everyone is funnier, more loveable, and even prettier when there's alcohol involved. If you don't drink, try Rescue Remedy, a homeopathic natural stress reliever that will help you cut that jagged edge.

Strategy 5: Be honest. I wouldn't advise you to have this conversation with your new girlfriend right out of the chute; let some time pass, let your relationship settle into place, let those floodgates of honesty be open for awhile, flowing freely, before you unload on her about BB. Remember, she really likes BB, so be careful with how you word things. And, most importantly, before you approach the subject, get a really good grip on why BB bugs. Telling her it's the way her lips move isn't going to cut it. Once you're honest, then it will not only be easier on you to dodge plans, but it may also make you feel better. Maybe your girl feels the same way? Yet, she can shine some light on BB's positive traits, helping you focus on something else besides her tiny lips.

When you love her friends

Even though Texas adores my friends, I've seen her roll her eyes at our shenanigans, and to be quite honest, I don't blame her—sometimes we can be really obnoxious.

Texas, who always has a glass of wine in her hand when they're around, typically laughs when someone takes her top off and launches it across the backyard, but she draws the line when one of us heads to the roof naked to do a cannonball into the pool. Texas laughs, tries to talk us down, and then makes sure the phone's handy to call 911 as she continues sipping her glass of red wine. It's no secret that we sometimes drive her crazy, or that she'd rather be kicking it with her friends, but she stays put in her lounge chair and smiles because this is what we do—we deal.

As different people, we surely have different tastes in friends and we surely have different thresholds for what we constitute as funny, responsible, and downright ridiculous. But, in the end, we have to try to soften our edges and meet in the middle when it comes to those we love and those they love.

DIPSTICK: When is your next sorority gathering, Lipstick? I can't wait to see you and your sisters jumping naked from the roof.

Lipstick: I'll keep you posted.

What about that friend of hers who acts like a jealous ex-girlfriend?

I had a friend named Sam (Selfish Awkward Manipulator) who used to sabotage my relationships. When I'd first meet a girl, Sam would be totally supportive. She'd bond with this new flame and we'd all hang out together. It wasn't until my relationship turned a corner—like we slept together or said I love you—that Sam began to raise her eyebrow. No matter what my new girl did, Sam didn't like it and it drove me crazy. I confronted her about it, but it was no use. "I just want you to be happy," she'd say. "Don't you want me to be honest?" These games persisted for some time. Not until years later, when a mutual friend shared that Sam secretly had feelings for me, did it all make sense.

DIPSTICK: These friends are the toughest to love. To them, nothing you do is right, so you stop trying so hard. Do your best to dodge their bullets and smile. That said, in our younger years, haven't we all been there, like Lipstick said? Even when you like your girlfriend's friends, sometimes they're just around too much. It's hard to work on your relationship and grow as a couple if there is always a buddy hanging around. Make it a point to plan a romantic weekend away from time to time, or set aside Sundays as your special days. That friend you always find on the couch? Set some boundaries. She can only stay one day a week, or once a month (or year), whatever feels right to you. You need to support your friends, but shit, they've got to learn to take care of themselves, too!

Whether you like her friends or not, honor who they are in her life and the history they share, or else . . .

Her Smell Is Still on the Sheets

Dealing with the ex-girlfriend(s)

What would you do in Nikki's shoes?

Nikki was checking her e-mail on Ann's computer when an instant message popped up. "Hi, hon. What are you doing home from work?" It was from Ann's ex, Brianna. Nikki was shocked. She had no idea Brianna and

Ann were still in touch. The only thing she knew about Brianna was how she trampled all over Ann's heart. Nikki was tempted to pretend to be Ann and converse with her, but decided against it. Still, how could she bring the topic up with Ann without her thinking she was snooping?

DIPSTICK: Unless this is her first lesbian relationship, chances are your new flame has an ex or two lurking in the shadows. Exes are a vital part of most lesbians' lives. She may have fond memories of the girl who brought her out, or she may be recovering from an ex from hell. As her new girlfriend, learning how to tactfully handle the ex-girlfriend is crucial to lesbian relationship success. Here are a few types of exes and how you can best deal with them.

The ex who wants your girl back

Every time Dipstick has ended a relationship, her ex has wanted her back. Sometimes days after the breakup, sometimes years, usually after I had moved on to someone else. This is common for lesbians. We always want what we can't have and appreciate someone more when they're gone. It's normal to feel threatened by an ex who wants your honey back. Just like women forget the pain of childbirth, we somehow forget the terrible things our ex girlfriends did. As her new lover, it is your job to set your girlfriend straight and remind her of every mean and awful thing her ex did. Keep a notebook so you'll remember. Then, when she pops up on your gal's IM, you'll be prepared with an arsenal of nasty things to fling her way.

Lipstick: Dip, maybe you can get everyone to gang up at recess and pull her hair by the drinking fountain, too?

DIPSTICK: Ex-girlfriends can mean war, Lipstick. You know this.
   While you're reminding her of how horrible her ex was, be sure to treat her like a princess. Hold the door, bring her flowers, and for St. Sappho's sake, be sure to keep her on cloud sixty-nine in the boudoir. Studies show that the chemicals released during orgasm slowly replace memories of previous sexual relations with new ones, so make sure the new memories count.

The ex who wants you (or your girl) dead

We've all been there. You're hanging out at the bar, having a great time, until SHE walks in. It's your new lover's ex. She glares in your direction, firmly plants herself at the bar, downing beer after beer, pausing only long enough to throw sharp stares your way. The minute your gal gets up to pee, the ex wobbles her drunken ass over to your table and starts saying you're an ugly whore and if you knew what was best for you, you'd leave "Suzy" alone. She clumsily swings and misses you, but lands a jab right in the belly of the basketball player walking by, drinks in hand. Cocktails and swear words are flying. What now, you ask. Take Dipstick's advice: Grab your jacket and your girl and get the hell out of Lavender Lounge.

Dealing with a disgruntled ex-lover is no fun. She can make your lover's life hell by making all kinds of unreasonable demands. For example: She wants your gal to pay half her car payment because they were together when she bought the car. Or she might withhold visitation of their cocker spaniel until your honey bunch returns the Go-Go's vinyl collection she took, which, of course, your girl insists is hers.

The first thing to understand is the problem isn't you. The ex is pissed because her girl has moved on and she's stuck in her pathetic little life all alone. If you run into one of these angry exes, the best thing to do is not to engage and be totally supportive of your new girlfriend, no matter what happened. If the ex seems really scary and you're truly worried about your girl's safety, encourage her to file a restraining order.

But more important than how you react is to observe how your new gal responds. If she seems intent on getting involved in the drama, take note. She may be addicted to the adrenaline rush that only a dysfunctional relationship can provide, and you know what that means: Once it runs the course with her ex, you're next!

Some lesbians spend their whole lives avoiding their ex-girlfriends. This isn't a good idea; it gives the ex too much power. It's best to be firm and clear with ex-lovers, and avoid being overly emotional or confrontational. Encourage your girl to stand her ground, to go on with life, and to hold her head up high.

When her ex is abusive

If your lady is escaping an abusive relationship, this is an extra tricky situation. Abusers usually go after their lovers, but sometimes they will also come after their ex's new flame. Because of this, both you and your partner should each have a plan. Whether that involves staying with a friend or relative or calling 911, make sure you're prepared if the looney strikes.

What makes a person abusive? Here are some warning signs of abuse. Has he (or she—remember battering is as common is same-sex relationships as opposite):

- hit your partner?
- threatened her with violence?
- used money to manipulate her?
- humiliated her in front of other people?
- tried to control her actions?
- threatened to out her to her family or job?
- threatened to hurt you, your pets, or your children?

If any of the above apply to you or your girlfriend, find a good professional domestic violence counselor.

The ex who is your girl's best friend

This is a tricky one. We all want to be with someone who gets along with her exes. Yet, sometimes we can't help but feel jealous of the intimacy and past they shared.

So what do you do with your feelings? Well, first you have to understand them. Are you threatened by their relationship? If so, you need to ask yourself why. Maybe you see the comfortable way they are together and it makes you wish you and your girl had that kind of connection. Perhaps you think she's prettier, smarter, or funnier than you are. If so, get a grip. Maybe she is, but you need to remember that they broke up for a reason. No matter her good qualities, she was not an ideal partner for your girlfriend, and as of right now you are so don't blow it!

Dipstick believes a strong offense is the best defense. Want to stay in your new girl's life? Become friends with her ex! Take your dogs out for a hike, invite her to your neighborhood barbeque, check out a concert together. Once you win over her favorite ex, you're in.

Lipstick: There's truth to what you're saying Dip, but you forgot some things. What about the *ex you want to sleep with?* What happens when you get a crush on your girlfriend's ex-girlfriend? How do you deal with that?

Surely it's happened to you—you're bonding at the dog park when you suddenly see that look in her eye? It's not intentional, but she's so damn hot in those yoga pants. If you find yourself in this predicament, curb how much time you're spending together. Forget bonding; focus on other things besides checking out her ass.

And something else you forgot to address, Dip: *What to do if your girlfriend doesn't have any exes?*

This is a red flag—not a huge one, but one to make note of. If she hasn't been around the lesbian block, there could be trouble because there are lots of hurdles, temptations, and road blocks in your first pass. Also, if the woman you're dating is fresh from the closet, beware. Don't fool yourself and think you're going to live happily ever after. You might, but that's a big might.

DIPSTICK: Right on, Lip. Be wary, but don't write her off completely. Sometimes people do find everlasting love with their first. Don't count on it, but you may be one of the lucky ones.

Who's That Man Beating on the Door?

Dealing with the men in their lives

Jenny and Carolyn were happy in the bliss of a new and sex-filled relationship. Jenny was spending the night at Carolyn's house when early the next morning, she was woken by loud banging and a man yelling outside their bedroom window. Jenny threw on her boxer shorts and T-shirt and followed Carolyn downstairs to find a scruffy man at the door asking Carolyn for the car keys. Jenny knew Carolyn had been with men in the past. It turns out this fellow was not just some man, but her husband. They were separated, but still married, and shared a car. Jenny was so upset she was about to leave the relationship until Carolyn convinced her she was only staying married for tax benefits and health insurance. Jenny has come to accept this fact, but still she wonders what other things Carolyn and her husband share and what impact this will have on their long-term relationship.

DIPSTICK: Everyone's partner has a past. Unfortunately, some are still living in it. Like Jenny, you may find yourself in love with a woman who was (or currently is) married to a man. Your new sweetie may still have a relationship with her ex-husband—especially when children are involved. This can bring up feelings of jealousy or insecurity. Or it may just take away from your time with your girlfriend. How do you navigate your new relationship when there are 200 pounds of hairy baggage attached?

First things first: No double dipping. Both Lipstick and I are very clear on this point. If someone is married, don't mess with her. Not only are you setting yourself up for heartbreak, you're also hurting an innocent third party.

Lipstick: And it's bad karma!

DIPSTICK: Lesbians can create enough drama on their own; you don't need to add a third person to the mix.

There are, of course, a few exceptions to this rule:

- If her husband knows about you and is OK with it. (Watch out for your heart!)
- She's in the process of getting a divorce and no longer lives with him.
- She married her husband for a green card and he's a bigger homo than you are.

Ex-husbands can be great, or they can be a pain in the ass. Sometimes they'll come over and help repair the Volkswagen or watch your dog when you're out of town. But others want to get between you and your sweetie (literally!). It's tricky to navigate the world of ex-husbandville.

Nontraditional families

Lipstick and I support all kinds of families. We love diversity and believe it makes our world a better place, but sometimes you can find yourself implicated in a relationship you didn't sign up for. When you start dating someone who has a good and strong relationship with her ex-husband, you can feel like the third wheel. We know lesbians who still live with their ex-husbands and children, each having their own relationships with new partners. Sometimes these relationships work out great, other times they're superconflicted.

Lipstick: I've never seen one work out.

DIPSTICK: Regardless, you need to determine what your role is or just stay out of it. If your partner asks your advice, then feel free to give it. Like her relationship with her parents or her children, she has to figure out what is the best path for her. She does not need you meddling into her affairs and telling her how to live her life.

If she is indeed married to him and having an affair with you—even though Lipstick & Dipstick warned you not to—your role is to be patient. If she is contemplating leaving her marriage to be with you, that is a big, life-changing step for her. You should be prepared to give her as much time and space as needed.

If she is taking too long and you can't wait for her, then you need to move on. Sure it may be heart breaking for the both of you, but this is a decision that can't be rushed. Her life will change forever.

For the sake of the kids

When you get involved with a woman who has children, there's one thing you need to understand: Her kids come first. For the sake of her children, she might decide to have a relationship with the children's father, but Lipstick & Dipstick do not believe children's best interests are served when the parents are unhappy closet cases.

When you're jealous of the ex-husband

There's a saying, made famous on *The L Word*: "Most women are straight, until they're not." When someone is newly out and still has dick on her breath, you may be concerned that lesbian lovemaking is not going to satisfy her. To this, Dipstick only has one thing to say: let it go. No man can compare to luscious labia-on-labia love.

Lipstick: I disagree. If your new girlfriend is newly out and "still has dick on her breath" then you should keep some guardrails up. And this (when you're jealous of the ex-husband), to me, is more about penis envy than jealousy.

DIPSTICK: Dipstick knows there's nothing more luscious than a girl's pink lips and can't imagine anyone leaving a loving honey's arms for the hard and hairy hands of a man. Yet, we acknowledge it does happen from time to time.

Lipstick: It happens a lot, D!

DIPSTICK: Whatever Lip, don't make me lose my momentum. If your latest lady truly is straight and is only dabbling in the furry taco, there is nothing you can do about it. Getting jealous and trying to control her isn't gonna help.

Other types of ex-boyfriends and ex-husbands

Men come in all types and sizes. Here are some quick tips on how to deal with various man-types.

Vinnie Velcro, who won't grant her a divorce because he just can't let go. The loser dude needs to grow up and get a life of his own.

Solution: Find a good lawyer.

Joe Lonely, who doesn't have a life. This hapless fellow doesn't have any friends and still relies on his ex-wife for his social interaction. He invites himself over for dinner, her out to the movies, and the both of you to go on vacation with him at his cabin.

Solution: While a few nights under the stars seems tempting, the best way to deal with this guy is to turn him down gently. Set him up with your coworker's sister.

Peeping Peter, who wants to watch. Let's face it, some guys are creepy. It can be harsh to realize the woman you're in love with was married to one of those cretins. You know the kind: when his wife came out to him, he got excited, hoping it meant she'd bring chicks home.

Solution: The best thing you can do is to stay far away from this guy. Even if you're into the whole threesome thing, I advise you to find a new boy toy, one who's not intimately connected to your prior life. There's just too much baggage with an ex-husband.

Right Wing Richard, also known as "The Dick." Yikes, we hate him. Whether he's a bible-beating hypocrite, a narrow-minded right winger, or a desperate closet case himself, this type of ex can be hard to handle.

Solution: Let him know that his wife left him, not because she is a lesbian, but because he was inadequate in bed. Who cares that this will only fuel his homophobic rage—these types never change anyway.

Groovy Gary, who's hip and down with his ex-wife being a dyke. At first you love this guy. He is so supportive of his wife's happiness that he considers you a part of his new family. He marches next to you in the Pride parade and writing pro-gay letters to the editor is his new hobby. We love this guy too . . . from afar.

Solution: He'd make a great politician. Get him to run for office.

Barry and Bimbo, the ex and his new wife. Now that you're each starting your own families, you may decide it's time you all became friends. We have no problem with this. Lesbians stay friends with their ex-girlfriends all the time, why should we exclude ex-husbands? Hell, go on vacation together for all we care, just as long as you're all having fun.

Solution: If you don't like them, try Xanax, Valium, or an over-the-counter sedative.

Lipstick: Dipstick, what about the ex-husband that's still her husband?

God bless lesbos who can date a woman who's still married. I'm not sure how they do it, but I do know that those relationships rarely last long. I've seen more than one train wreck in my years. I had one friend who started seeing a woman who was still married, but "only legally" she claimed. "Her husband knows all about us and they're just staying married until their kids get out of high school."

Give me a break, I thought, smiling and only giving my enormous opinion if she asked. Naturally—knowing intuitively that she's driving through a railroad crossing while ignoring the flashing stop signs—she doesn't ask.

So, I'll give it to you instead: Either shit or get off the pot.

To the ladies out there who are still married, Lipstick believes there are no good excuses to keep that marriage certificate if you're no longer in a relationship. I understand it's circumstantial—family, the closet, your job, whatever—but if you'd like to be a grown-up lesbian and enter into a relationship of your own, you've gotta lose the hubby and shred that legal document.

There are a number of reasons staying married is a bad idea. The first, and the most important, is the control issue—he will always have a psychological, legal, and possibly emotional stronghold on the wife, no matter how dykey she is or how much she loves poon. There is no room for a serious girlfriend, one who wants to become completely enmeshed in your life, with a demanding husband around.

The second reason is it's a total turnoff. There's no better way to send women running (in the opposite direction) than for them to hear you're still married with no divorce on the horizon.

It's pretty simple, girls, most lesbians want monogamy—just the two of you cozy in a cabin in the woods, *sans* the husband!

My Girlfriend's Dad Is a Spineless Homophobe

Dealing with her family

Latisha and Fern had been dating for five years, but Fern had never met Latisha's parents. When Latisha came out to her folks, they threw her out of the house and told her to only return when she had recovered from her sinful ways. It had taken Latisha some time to rebuild a relationship with her family, but one thing they never discussed was her being a lesbian. There was an unspoken understanding that certain things were not talked about. Because Fern's parents had practically thrown her a party when she came out, she couldn't understand what the big deal was. She was certain that if she met Latisha's family and they saw how happy she and Latisha were together, they would begin to accept their lesbian daughter.

When her parents are homophobes

DIPSTICK: When we come out to our parents, sometimes the conversation goes like this:

Big Dyke: Mom, I have something to tell you.
Mom: Oh, no. Don't even tell me you're knocked up.
Big Dyke: No, no Mom, it's nothing like that.
Mom: Because when your cousin Alice had that baby out of wedlock, you know who was stuck raising the child. Your Aunt Thelma and Uncle Ernesto. Don't think for a moment that I'm going to raise some dirty-diapered bastard baby.
Big Dyke: You've got it all wrong. I'm a lesbian.
Mom: A lesbian! Then how did you get pregnant?

Some parents go ballistic when one of their children comes out. Others have a hard time, but gradually come around and accept and even embrace their child's homosexuality. In rare instances, some parents are thrilled when little Joanie declares herself a dyke.

If you come from a supportive family, it can be hard to understand what someone from the other side of the tracks is going through.

Like Latisha, you may feel it's more important to have a less-than-ideal relationship with your parents, rather than force them to accept you're gay. While this may seem like a perfect compromise to you, only you know how far your parents are willing to bend; this may be confusing or difficult for your partner to understand.

Every dyke has a different relationship with her family. Some of us grow up in abusive households, in broken families, or in a religion that doesn't accept homosexuality. Some of us had a strained relationship even before we came out. The harm some of us suffered at the hands of our families is nothing to make light of. But then, some of our parents encouraged us, were our biggest cheerleaders growing up, and continue to support our life choices. Most of us fall somewhere in the middle.

No matter how contentious or heartening, we each love our family in our own way. We accept their faults (or don't) and they accept ours (or don't). But what happens when your girlfriend tries to tell you how to handle your family? If there's one thing Dipstick would never put up with, it's a partner who tries to tell me how I should and shouldn't be with my family.

Sure, you can help your girlfriend process her relationships. Be there for her, love her, give her an outsider's perspective—but you should never interfere. Don't invite her homophobic mother over for breakfast behind your girlfriend's back. Don't call her brother and tell him he should let his sister see her nieces, or that she's not going to make them gay. And don't nag your partner, trying to fit her into some parental/daughter relationship mold of how you think things should be.

Lipstick: I'd like to add that you'd also best be leery when talking trash about homophobic kin. Even though they may be horrible to you or your honey pie and she may say she hates them, you should never, ever agree with her. Listen, encourage, try to be positive, and if none of that's possible, then keep your trap shut. No matter how nasty they are, they're still her blood.

Hypothetical Lover: I can't believe my dad just kicked you out of our house for talking about your gay column during dinner. I'm so sorry he's such a homophobic prick!

Lipstick (crying): I know. How could he do that? And call me those things. And throw my purse into the yard like that?

Hypothetical Lover: It's going to be fine. He didn't mean that you were fat. He just meant that you have big bones.

Lipstick: He called me a pig-faced lard ass.

Hypothetical Lover: Well, he's ignorant and a total moron. Ignore him.

Lipstick: You're right. Why should I be crying just because he's an ignorant asshole?

Hypothetical Lover: Whoa. Don't call my dad an asshole! How dare you talk about my family like that!

DIPSTICK:

When your girlfriend wants your family more than you

I once had a girlfriend, Bette, who came from a broken home. Her father left when she was young and her mom suffered from mental illness. She was raised by distant relatives. When I brought Bette home to my family, she immediately fell in love. My parents, brothers, and sisters were all welcoming. She adored my mom, who baked her cookies and invited her to dinner. When I broke up with Bette, I didn't know who she was going to miss more—me or my mom. Whenever I'd see Bette out at the bar, she'd always ask about Mom, but never how I was.

Lipstick: That's because you dumped her ass.

DIPSTICK: You're probably right. Regardless, there was nothing wrong with Bette falling for my family, but it was *my* family. I had my own history and relationship with them. It only became a problem when Bette wanted to put my family before our relationship. She would ask to pop over on the weekends and invited my parents to lesbian parties at her apartment. Can you believe that?

I didn't mind sharing my family with Bette. Even I'll admit they're pretty cool people, but there had to be limits. Know yours and be sure to express them if your girlfriend steps across the line.

When her parents head up the local PFLAG chapter

Whenever the PFLAG contingent marches by in the Gay Pride parade, I always overhear someone lamenting how she wishes her parents were that supportive. I usually witness at least one queer crying, mournful about "what might have been" with his family.

Sure, having PFLAG parents would be great, but I've seen the other side of this, as well. Pamela was a young lesbian, entering her senior year of high school, when she came out to her mom. Pamela was very active in her school's gay/straight alliance and was a member of the high school debate team. She either wanted to be a lawyer or run an animal rescue organization when she was done with college. With much support from her gay/straight alliance peers, equipped with PFLAG brochures, Pamela came out to her mother. Her mom, who was not utterly surprised to learn of her daughter's proclivities, went to a PFLAG meeting to see what it was all about. The next thing Pamela knew, her mom was heading up the "Parents of Teenagers" contingent of the local chapter, holding meetings in their living room and trying to get herself invited to Pamela's gay/straight alliance to offer support to those whose parents didn't. Her mom took to writing letters to the editor of the local paper and even campaigned door-to-door against an anti-gay marriage amendment. Leaving lesbian safe-sex pamphlets on her bed was the last straw. "I haven't even had a girlfriend yet! I just wish my mom would get a life of her own!" Pamela screamed to her gay/straight alliance peers.

Poor Pamela. None of her friends understood. They all just wished they had a mom as cool as hers. When you're faced with a mom who wants you to be her poster child, there are only two things you can do. (1) Pretend to be straight or (2) introduce your mom to a cause she's even more likely to fall deep into, like the Kitten Amputee Society.

Lipstick: If your mom reminds you of Sharon Gless from *Queer as Folk*—with or without the kitschy bling—how about just leveling with her? Tell Mom that even though you love her and appreciate that she's so supportive, you'd like her to bring it down a notch. Just a notch though, not all together. We mustn't squelch her burning flame, as we need all the help we can get!

DIPSTICK:

When her parents act like you don't exist

When faced with an over-exuberant PFLAG mom, the parent who acts like you don't exist can seem like a blessing. This dad walks right past you in your own home, opens the fridge, and rummages for a beer. You're not invited to family barbeques and when her mom calls, she never says hello, just, "Is Stacy home?" You try your darnedest, attempting to engage in conversation and even invite them over for an elaborate meal. After slaving for hours in the kitchen, they stuff their faces without so much as a word and then quickly retreat to the living room to catch the end of a baseball game.

These people are just rude and I think you're lucky if your partner escaped with any manners at all. Even the most virulent of homophobic talk show hosts would thank a lesbian for a home-cooked meal. My advice: do anything you can to get noticed. Ride your motorcycle through her mother's patch of prized roses, show up at the family reunion in full leather with your girlfriend on a leash, or start dry humping your lover on the dance floor at cousin Flo's wedding. You might not win your way into their graces, but at least the family will be forced to acknowledge you.

Dipstick's Quiz: Are You Ready for I Love You?

1. Which relationship most resembles yours:
    a. lesbian first love like in *The Incredibly True Adventures of Two Girls in Love*.
    b. secretive and frantic, like Jenny and Marina in the first season of *The L Word*.
    c. felonious like lesbian serial killer Aileen Wournos and her naive lover Tyria Moore in *Monster*.

2. You've met:
    a. her parents.
    b. her whole softball team.
    c. how can I meet anyone, we don't leave the bedroom!

3. When you're not in bed, you're most likely to be:
    a. staring into each other's eyes over a slow dinner and good glass of wine.
    b. off with your friends, doing your own thing.
    c. not in bed?

4. On your first vacation you:
    a. went with her on the trip to Hawaii she had planned with her ex-lover before they broke up.
    b. didn't go with her to Provincetown—you were in Atlantic City with your ex because you were too guilty about the breakup to cancel the trip.
    c. haven't gone on vacation yet, but you did go to a movie that was filmed in Paris.

5. When you're not with her:
    a. you're daydreaming of dripping orange popsicle all over her body and licking it off.
    b. not with her? We're always together!
    c. you're flirting with the cute FedEx driver.

6. She broke up with her last lover:
    a. last year.
    b. last week.
    c. she's still with him.

7. The two of you met:
    a. at an indoor soccer tournament. She scored a goal on you.

  b. online—after weeks of IM and e-mail. You haven't met in person yet.

  c. in the office—she's your therapist.

8. Every time you make love:

  a. we're saving ourselves for gay marriage.

  b. she screams your name in ecstasy.

  c. she's drunk.

9. After your first date you:

  a. kissed her good night at her door.

  b. moved in.

  c. by date, do you mean we've left the bedroom?

10. How much do you know about her?

  a. a lot! We talk about everything.

  b. I know her last name starts with an R.

  c. I saw a glimpse of her cable bill on the table on my way out one morning. She's got Showtime.

Add it up.

a = 2 points
b = 1 point
c = 0 points

6 Points or Fewer: Tomcat

You are nowhere near ready to take this girl out to dinner, let alone tell her you love her. Go back to bed and enjoy the great sex, while you're still having it. There will be plenty of time for "I love you" four years down the road when you're fighting about the lack of sex in your relationship.

7–14 Points: Pussy-Footing Kitties

You and your gal are moving in the right direction, but you're not quite ready to declare your amore yet. Wait a bit. Maybe she'll say it first.

15 Points or More: Purring Kittens

Congratulations! It's time to pop. Light the candles, set the mood, and look directly into her eyes when you say, "I love you."

Lipstick: Acknowledge you in the police lineup. They're not just rude, Dipstick, they're in denial and totally out of touch with their own sexuality. Those people who are most homophobic are those who are terrified of their own fantasies, the ones that not only get them off, but those that they would *never* admit to. Don't take Dipstick's advice and tear up her mother's rose bushes; instead, kill them with kindness. Don't give them a reason to dislike you. Send them positive energy and don't allow them to belittle you. After all, what closet-case queen Eleanor Roosevelt said is true: "No one can make you feel inferior without your consent."

When your gaydar goes off

There's nothing worse than finally meeting the parents, only to have your gaydar go off when you shake hands. Ding Ding Ding. Either the dad loves your handbag, or it's clear your girl got her chops from Mom. She had to have picked up the gene somewhere. Worse yet would be that they're both moes who have somehow found each other—in confidence or in denial—and decided to live together in sickness and in health.

No matter what you're faced with when it comes to family, remember these three things:

1. Be friendly
2. Be gracious, and when all else fails
3. Be quiet.

PART II

Cohabitating

CHAPTER FOUR

Moving in Together

S o, you've said I love you and you've decided you want to grow old together. Now what? How about moving in together? But wait! Before you call the moving truck, take the time to dig into this chapter so you know what to expect. Start with Lipstick's Preliminary Pussy Period, so you can determine if you're jumping the gun. Dipstick's Moving Tips will help you navigate the uprooting process. After that, we will offer advice for those first few months under the same roof. These topics include grooming, housekeeping, and dealing with children, even the furry ones.

Lipstick's Preliminary Pussy Period (a.k.a. Triple P)

So, you are in loooooooooooove. You're certain she's the one and you want to spend the rest of your lives together. Lipstick's happy for you, but before you pack up your things or make room in your closet for her clothes, I highly recommend you follow my Preliminary Pussy Period (Triple P)—a four-step process before cohabitating. It's simple and relatively painless, and applying this to your life will increase your chances of creating fruitful, long-term lesbian love, a kinship free of codependency and regrets.

Why, you ask, can't we just move in together and start our lives? We're in love and even though we've only known each other for two weeks, we're soul mates and I've never loved anyone more.

Well, sister, there's a good reason to follow Lipstick's Triple P: you just can't be responsible when you're under the influence of *cunnilingus crack*. We've all been there, the sex-crazed narcosis we're thrown into when we fall in love. Beyond experiencing it ourselves, the most poignant perspective we have is when one of our friends tries to go about her daily life amidst her crack-induced stupor. It's a debilitating drug whose effects are myriad. It makes your best friend fall off the face of the earth for months, do things she'd never do when solo and sober—like couple's ballroom dancing, forty-eight-hour stints of silent Kama Sutra, at which point she and her new girlfriend only sober up enough from their love potion to drive to the store for the staples they've been living on: lube and chocolate syrup. Seeing them at the market can be jarring—that glazed look in their eyes, the way they can't be bothered with anyone else around them, giggling like children when picking up the Super Bowl Nerf ball stand they knocked over.

It's not their fault; it's not anyone's fault. The hard fact is that we have no control over how or what our libido injects into our bloodstream, the boobilcious juices that inhibit our better judgment during this time period. What we do have control over is the catch systems we put into place before we slide into this lustful la-la land. Enter Lipstick's Triple P, a road map for the dazed and cuntfused that, once fully integrated into your lesbian psyche, will give you some perspective and help you make the best choices when under the influence.

Step 1: Embrace the Dyke Gestation Period (DGP) (six months). It's super-important to have a period of time in the beginning of your relationship—a minimum of six months—to simply date and enjoy falling in love. Sleepovers. Date nights. Breakfast in bed. Late night carpet picnics. You'll probably shut out the rest of the world—only coming up for air to get groceries and go to work.

During the DGP, there are many things to contemplate. Beyond her great rack and that one little thing you never knew you liked in bed, there are many things to consider before taking the plunge and moving in together. Leases and mortgages and capital gains; sleeping habits, cleanliness, and boundaries; there are roommates, animals, and, in some cases, even children to consider. Let this DGP run its course or you might end up having a serious overdose and needing rehab by the time the U-Haul pulls away from the curb.

We've practically been living together, you say, so why not get our own place right away?

Because Lipstick said so. Trust me on this one. If you were starving (not literally, but superhungry like after a long day working at the Pride festival with no food), would you rather have a greasy cheeseburger as you're walking to your car, or wait a tad longer until you get home, where you could have a big fat cut of filet mignon?

DIPSTICK INTERJECTION: Lip, poor analogy. The new find may be the filet. The reason to wait is to see if you're really a filet girl or, if like my cousin Chauncey, you actually do prefer hamburger.

Step 2: Tryouts (three months). After the six month DGP, it's time to make some preliminary decisions. Whose place should you inhabit while you're going through tryouts? During this three-month period, you'll be trying each other on, making sure that you're compatible under the same roof. No matter where you live, it's important to give your domestic energy a few months to balance out before signing a lease or buying a home together.

If you're not quite ready to cohabitate (either emotionally or physically), then a good alternative to tryouts is *heavy immersion*, which is, essentially tryouts on steroids. You don't live together, but you're together so much—taking turns where you sleep and watch your movies—that your neighbors think you're roommates. Heavy immersion includes her own set of toiletries at your house, a decent-size space in your closet for a few spare jammies and panties, as well as the goodies she likes on the shelves and in the fridge.

Step 3: House Hunting (two months). Once the DGP is behind you, as well as tryouts, you can start hunting for a little love shack of your own to rent or buy. Lipstick believes it's *very* important to eventually get a place of your own, one that is yours and yours only, free of ex-girlfriend energy. Remember, if you buy together, it's important to be protected in case one of you dies—ask your mortgage broker about the right of survivorship. If you're in any way second-guessing the big move, then I'd encourage you to sit still and wait a few more months until you're sure.

This four-step process is easily extendable, but not to be curtailed for any reason.

Step 4: Nesting (Forever). Mmmmm. The best part. If there's any way you can swing it logistically, I always like to move into a new place mid-September. This gives you fall (my favorite season) to begin nesting and all of winter to ensure that the each room in the house is not only christened, but also really feels like home. This phase is essential in building a healthy, happy home. If you're out at the bars whooping it up with your friends or at a different summer BBQ each night, then it will take longer to settle in. Get to know the way her feet sound against the hardwood floors and how both of you best fit in that claw-foot tub.

If, and only if, you make it through my Triple P can you consider taking your relationship to the next level: getting a cat, walking down the aisle, or having children. Be wise and don't jump the gun.

Dipstick's Moving Tips

1. That blanket in the back of the truck is to wrap around her valuables, not for a nap.
2. The ramp does not double as a skateboard ramp.
3. Don't dolly race when her grandmother's antique dresser is on board.
4. Your friend Jo may be a great quarterback, but she probably shouldn't have beamed that crystal vase to Butterfinger Betty.
5. Serve the pizza and beer *after* you're done moving.
6. Don't let your mother pack up your bedroom.
7. One plunger is plenty. And they probably don't want your old one at the Goodwill.
8. Don't forget to go back for her cat.
9. Set the bedroom up first, but wait to christen it until your friends have left.
10. Don't forget to call everyone of those gals on the volleyball team *you* helped move.

I Love Everything about Her, But . . .

Dirty panties, stinky breath, and hogging the covers

Picture this: You're dating some hottie who's perfect for you. She's smart, intellectually stimulating, has a job she loves, and donates time to worthy causes . . . but she picks her teeth with the steak knife after dinner and when she laughs, small children cry because of the high-pitched squealing noise. Worse yet, she has halitosis!

What do you do when you're really into someone and you think everything is great about her, except that one little thing?

Lipstick: If this is where you find yourself, odds are you haven't exchanged I love yous. And if you have, you didn't mean it unconditionally, or in the same way I love Texas. Her dirty panties don't bother me; neither does her morning breath. Not much she does bothers me. The contrary, actually. I love these things, for they make her who she is. Don't get me wrong, however, there are times when something she does irritates me—the way she occasionally leaves a trail of clothes from the front door to the bedroom.

Something else that involves unconditional love is dealing with private bathroom time.

It's a defining moment in any relationship—the first fart. The cry of an imprisoned turd naturally and eventually leads to the quintessential poop, which, I should add, should always be followed by the quintessential match.

Like passing gas, or your chicken bento from the day before, typically, the movement from the first boopsy (fart) to actually "dropping the kids off at the pool" is relatively smooth. But that's not true for everyone. There are lots of reasons for this.

The first is our good old friend denial. "How could something so gross come from my beautiful girlfriend? There's no way she poops," you say. And then you accidentally go into the bathroom after her one morning, and suddenly, as you're sitting on the toilet pinching your nose, you must face the harsh reality—yes, that hot little ass that you like to slap does indeed drop hellacious bombs. If you're not careful, and your denial is especially strong, then this premature realization can be really jarring.

The second reason for this impasse is your own discomfort with poop. If you're not ready to admit you pinch loaves, and hide your visits to the john as merely peeing, then you're sure as hell not ready to know about her BMs. The book *Everybody Poops* is a good place for you to start.

Beyond bodily functions you deal with and the idiosyncrasies you adore, can you get past other serious, gnawing issues?

It depends.

Superficial-califragilisticexpialidocious

This is the ever-so-powerful tapping on our brain that makes us give a shit what others think. These are the things that bother you about your new girl because you're afraid (consciously or subconsciously) what your friends will think. These issues include:

Noises. Do the things that come out of her body annoy you (save words, unless you don't like her voice)? A grating laugh is most common, but snorting in public is a close second. You're embarrassed by not only what your friends think, but complete strangers at the video store.

Personal style. Do you hate the clothes she wears? Women with vastly different styles don't usually make it on the first date (unless they meet at a pool party), but if they do, they're usually shocked when they see each other for the first time. Linen capris and a halter top don't always fancy flannel button-downs and 501s.

DIPSTICK: What? You think us 501ers want to date ourselves? I have nothing against a sexy lady in linen, but girls I hope you're not so shallow as you can't see past the pants and into her panties . . . I mean heart.

Lipstick: Where was I?

Hairstyle. Have you never seen such a long mullet? The old dyke hairstyles are tough to shake. This can be especially challenging for you older dykes who are into younger women.

Facial hair. Does her mustache rub your upper lip raw? This can be not only frustrating, but also painful.

Mode of transport. I know it seems ridiculous on paper, but some people care how you get around. Did you have dreams of your girl picking you up in her sexy black Range Rover, only to have her pull up in a beat-up Pinto? Or maybe she doesn't even have a car, only a bike, and she wants to ride Laverne and Shirley style.

DIPSTICK: Lip, are you really that shallow? Rejecting a girl for what kind of car she drives? Oh wait, I once refused to date a girl because she drove a Hummer, but that's because she was clueless of the impact the gas guzzler had on the environment.

Lipstick: I'm not saying I'd kick her to the curb because of her ride, but there are a lot of people who would be swayed by that. All of the superficial things above can be worked through if you're willing to look past them enough to get to know her.

Mirror, mirror on the wall

The problems you have with her are typically issues you also have with yourself. You say it drives you crazy that she has to pick the movies you see, but that's only because you're the biggest control freak in the world. These issues generally include:

Selfishness. If you're a selfish person, you know it and you hate seeing it in other people because it reminds you how ugly it is.

Center of attention. Do you love the spotlight? So does she? Big problem.

The iceberg

"Iceberg, right ahead!"

Remember that scene in *Titanic* when the two guys in the lookout first see the iceberg in the ominous distance? This is similar to what Lipstick sees when her friends meet someone with whom there are BIG roadblocks that scream, it ain't gonna work! This ship's gonna sink. These icebergs include:

Social graces. Did she not thank your mom for the dinner? Did she not leave a tip for the waitstaff? There are definite deal breakers in the beginning of a relationship associated with social graces.

Manners. Does she burp at the table? Fart in public? Grounds for the boot.

DIPSTICK: Are these manners or class differences? Not all of us were raised knowing which fork to use when and how to properly greet a lady. Not all of us were debutantes, Lipstick. Expelling pent-up gas is a natural and healthy thing to do. If you want to suffer with bloating and stomach distress, just to keep some strangers from being embarrassed, that's your issue. Dipstick says, "Let her rip!"

Lipstick: Farting in line at Saks Fifth Avenue is not OK. And I didn't say anything about forks.

Personality. After you're with her, are you all riled up? Is there something that leaves you on edge? Slightly perturbed? Anxietal? It's best to avoid people who are loud and aggressive because they suck you dry. Is she Debbie Downer—wah waaaaaah—and always looking at the negative side of things? This type of personality will also cause much distress and it will drag you down. Avoid women like that, too.

DIPSTICK: Debbie Downer I can agree with, but some of us are attracted to loud and aggressive women, Lipstick. I never had so much fun as when I dated Shanna, a big New Jersey gal, with lots of hair, lots of attitude, and lots of heart. She put me in my place, tied me to her bedposts, and let me have it. Sometimes I still have dreams of her . . .

What I guess I'm getting at is, it takes all kinds to make the dyke world go round. Be open to someone a little different than yourself—even if something initially bugs you—and you might find a whole new universe opened to you.

Bawling Babies

When your girl has kids

Lipstick: When you're a parent, kids are numero uno, and you'd better understand that before you get involved with a woman who has birthed a babe. If you're not interested in being a parent, or a parental figure for that matter, then don't get tangled up with a mom.

From all the letters we receive from women on this topic, here are a few of Lipstick's observations:

You gotta like kids. As I noted above, if you're not a kid person, you'd best not invest emotionally in the relationship. There's a chance, I suppose, that they could grow on you, but be very honest with yourself if your knee-jerk reaction was to frown when she first told you about them.

They don't have to like you. It can be a tough pill to swallow, but sometimes you have to accept that her kids are bitter about you. One thing to remember though: no matter what, you've got to respect them.

Figure out your role. Depending on what her family looks like, you'll have to find your spot. This can be tricky business when dealing with other parents, especially another territorial dyke who resembles a pit bull. The ex-husband is one thing; another mother will do anything (and I mean anything) when she feels threatened. Beware.

Learn to share. Having kids is all about sharing. Sharing your time, your girlfriend, your home, your intimate space, your bathroom, and as the child grows up, perhaps your makeup, your clothes, or your car. Unfortunately, all too often, this is the straw that breaks the lesbian's back. And let me tell you why . . .

The tricky thing about lesbian relationships is that they're so intense, especially in the beginning. When we first fall in love, the cunnilingus crack gives us tunnel vision—we are all we see. It doesn't matter how much you love your children, or how devoted you are to them, when you're bitten by the lesbo lovebug, you're instantly a hypnotized crack whore and she is all you want. During this time, it's very challenging to be apart and it's equally challenging to share your time. This serious obsessive hypnotism can be rudely shattered by work—having to put in forty hours away from your love can be brutal. And it can also throw a wrench in family time. It's kind of tough to have a moment on the couch when her three-year-old is tugging at your pant leg.

DIPSTICK: Lipstick is right. When your partner has kids already, the first thing you have to understand is that you're not going to be her number one priority. At least not until the youngins either go to college, turn eighteen, or join the army. Weaving a life together with someone who has a child is like any stepparent relationship. You love your partner first and foremost and hopefully you'll come to love her children. Before you move in together, you need to decide if you'll have a parenting role or if you'll just be another adult figure in the house. The children may have another parent already and not want or need a third.

The biggest no-no is moving in too quickly. Following Lipstick's Triple P is especially important here. For every partner who moves in and out, you'd better deposit $1,000 into your child's future therapy fund. Cha-ching. When you do determine it's time to move in together and become a big happy family, be ready for the kids to resent you for the attention you take away from them. It's nothing personal, so cut the kids some slack, OK? They're just needy chitlins looking for love and acceptance.

If you both have kids. When you both come together with children, this may seem like it is simpler, but actually, it's more complicated. You've now got two (or more) parents, different parenting styles, and children who may or may not get along.

The first thing you have to decide is what each parent's responsibility will be. Are you each going to parent each other's children, or will you only be Mom to your own kids? If you decide you're both going to be parents, be warned!

Having a new mother come in and start throwing her weight around too quickly can cause any aged child to rebel. The younger the child, the easier the adjustment. Heaven forbid you have a house full of teenagers. Dipstick thinks you should keep separate households if the kids involved are over twelve. It will just be smoother in the long run and in six short years, the kids will be gone and you can move in together.

Having another stable adult in their lives can be good for children. The operative word is *stable*. Don't expect things to work out effortlessly, but with good communication and support of each other, and perhaps a family counselor, you too can become the Brady Bunch.

And while children do come first, don't forget to put your relationship second. Get a babysitter and check out the date nights section of this book, Do You Come Here Often?

CHAPTER FIVE

Braiding Your Lives Together

I t can be fun to braid your lives together, but with that fun comes challenges if you're set in your ways. You like the fabric softener you use. You like which cabinet you keep your flatware in, which drawer your gloves and winter hats are in. You get off on how your checkbook balances and you can't imagine what a big Doberman pinscher would do to your hardwood floors. Well, get ready for things to change when you move in together. While sex-filled and exciting, cohabitating has its trials and tribulations. In this section, Lipstick & Dipstick help you navigate your new world with helpful tips, warnings, and suggestions.

Those Jeans Make You Look Fat

Honesty

"It's hard to believe that someone is telling the truth when you know that you would lie in his place."

—Henry Louis Mencken

DIPSTICK: Has your lover ever asked you, "Honey, do I look fat in these jeans?" How do you answer such a question, especially if they aren't the most flattering jeans? Yes, honesty is important in a relationship, but so is discretion. Dipstick learned this the hard way.

As Tiger approached thirty, she was having issues with getting older. Sprinkles of gray were showing up in her hair and the slightest hint of wrinkles were encroaching her eyes when she smiled. Personally, I loved it and thought it made her look distinguished and sexy. One day she came to me and asked, "Do you think I should dye my hair to cover up this gray?" It didn't seem like that big of a deal to me, so I told her she might look a little younger if she did. "I look old," she whined. "And I saw you checking out the waitress. Well, I've got news for you—she's going to get old one day, too."

Ouch.

We can all agree that honesty is a good thing, but like any good thing, too much of it can cause trouble. The key to being honest in any relationship is to know your partner's tender spots and don't ever, ever poke at them. Here are Dipstick's guidelines for how to be honest, but not too honest, in your relationship:

Tell the truth. Dipstick believes in being honest. It's what's my reputation is founded on and has gotten me the respect of people in high places. I usually don't hesitate to say exactly how I feel. Some people hate that about me, and honestly, I just don't care. Those who appreciate the candor are the people I call friends. One thing I can say is, you always know where you stand with me, because I don't sugarcoat the truth.

When you lie, you have to remember too much about what you said to whom. If you want to be a strong person, confident, and respected, speak your truth.

Lipstick: An exception here would be when you're in the closet. Then, and only then, is it OK to be dishonest . . . for awhile, but only if you're working toward getting out of the closet. If you're starting to put down roots in that dark space, then I've got a problem with you being a liar.

A friend of mine broke up with her girlfriend because she refused to come out. "I'm gonna do it," she'd say, over and over again, pacifying my friend into another few months; however, once some substantial time passed, it became glaringly obvious the girl had no intention of standing in her truth. It is OK to be a liar in the closet for awhile as you're getting comfortable in your new skin—we've all been there—but not for too long.

DIPSTICK: Wrong, Lipstick. It's never a good idea to knowingly be dishonest—especially when it comes to something as integral as our sexuality.

Lipstick: Exactly, Dipstick, it's an intimate, organic part of who we are, so it can be scary as hell when we first realize we like the taste of pussy. It's like "Uh oh!" Lipstick believes that being alone in your anxiety is OK. Necessary, actually. Not everyone is like you, Dipstick, and knew they were gay in the crib. It surprises some of us once we get through the layers and layers of denial. If it does, I believe you must come out to yourself slowly and then take even more time coming out of the closet to the world. Telling white lies along the way—like when Grandma asks what your new boyfriend's name is at Christmas dinner (you don't have to tell her it's Jennifer)—is OK.

For you closet dwellers out there: do it in your own time, but don't expect some stellar girlfriend to put up with your shady dealings for long. Losing her might be the price you'll have to pay.

DIPSTICK:

Don't be honest when it hurts. If there's one lesson I've learned in my life it's not to be honest when it hurts (either you or her) and there's no payoff. For example, you might think your girlfriend looks like a clown in that red lipstick, but where is telling her that going to get you? Certainly not any favors in bed. You'll only hurt her feelings and piss her off.

If you really hate the fact that she smokes, however, and you wish she would stop, then go ahead and make it known!

Lipstick: Little Texas, I promise to tell you if your new shade of MAC makes you look like Bozo.

DIPSTICK:

Complimentary lies are OK. Once, a few years ago, I had an important presentation at work. Wouldn't you know it, right before the big day, I got a huge cold sore on my upper lip. You know the kind that is red, sticks two feet out from your face, and oozes yellow goo.

Lipstick: Gross!

DIPSTICK: Everyone within a mile radius can't help but stare at it and whisper behind their hands to their friends. I stood in front of the mirror that morning, moaning, "Why me, why today?" I felt like shit and wanted to call in sick to work. Tiger grabbed my shoulders, looked me straight in the eye, and said, "Oh, honey, it doesn't look that bad." She lied. I knew it at the time, but somehow her words got me out the door and through my presentation. After I got home, I pulled all the blinds and hid in the basement until it was gone.

Sometimes we all need a little push and a white lie is all it takes to get us moving. Another example:

"You've got a good start to this article."
"Yes, it looks like you're losing weight."
"Great job on those cabinets! Now hand me my skill saw and let's just make a teeny tiny adjustment."

Never say what you truly feel about her mamma and her cooking. There are certain questions, when asked, you avoid answering, or, at the very least, avoid being honest. Here is a handful:

"How's the tempeh stir-fry?"
"What did your mother say about me?"
"Do you think she's more attractive than me?"
"Isn't my nephew sweet?"
"Did you ever come here with your ex-girlfriend?"

Never answer these. They're trick questions and will always backfire.

Lipstick: I'll add a few more:

"Should I get my boobs done?"
"Why didn't you eat all the dinner I made?"
"Did you have fun with my family at Christmas?"
"Do you think my hair is getting thinner?"

DIPSTICK:

If she asks, it's fair game. With the exception of the questions above, Dipstick believes that when people ask for your opinion, they really want to know. When I ask Lipstick for feedback on my writing, I want her to tell me what parts are funny, what parts suck, and what parts totally need to be rewritten. When I ask, I'm prepared for the answer. I ask because I'm stuck and I need guidance or because I value her opinion and want to hear it. I treat others who ask my advice the same way. Hell, I didn't become an advice columnist by dancing around the truth. I tell it like I see it, and you should, too.

Are You Sisters?

Enmeshment

Lesbian Twins. Do you know this couple? You've met them ten times, but you can never remember which one is Sharon and which one is Susan. They have the same salt-and-pepper hairstyle, the same khakis, and each wears a handmade vest bought at the women's craft festival. They have the same brand of trail shoes and matching raincoats in different colors. This couple has fallen into the lesbian enmeshment trap, and if you're not careful, you'll end up there, too.

DIPSTICK: But we're butch/femme, you say. It could never happen to us. Au contraire fine lesbian. I have seen couples unwittingly show up at lesbian fundraisers in the butch/femme version of the same outfit. Cowboy boots (men's and women's), one in Wranglers, the other in Levis, and a cowboy/girl shirt with bolo tie to top it off. Dykes, look at yourselves! Wearing the same clothes is just a symptom of what the experts like to call lesbian enmeshment.

Lipstick: Aside from wearing matching clothing, which I agree, is a homo no-no (see my fashion advice for couples), the urge to merge isn't all bad. There are just as many pros as there are cons. Think of all the clothes that Sharon and Susan get to share. I bet they have fights over who gets to wear the orange Womyn's Festival T-shirt on Halloween, even though they have it in four other colors. And some salons may give twofers for two people with the same haircut.

DIPSTICK: Be that as it may, Lip, it's up to each dyke to find a healthy balance of time together, time apart. Here are some things they need to understand.

Every relationship has three distinct parts:

1. *Separate time: I've got to earn a living.* This is when the two of you go about your lives, not really thinking or doing for the other. It's you time.
2. *Coming together: Please pass the salt.* This is where you come together to have dinner or call each other at work.
3. *Fusion: Honey, you're squishing my arm.* This is intimate time, when you intensely focus on each other.

Every relationship needs all three elements to be healthy.

Lipstick: Yawn, Dipstick. What are you, a counselor? Oh, right. You are. There are two other parts you forgot to mention:

4. *Fantasy land: I was daydreaming about someone else.* This is when you get caught up in a daydream and you forget you have a partner, or when you're masturbating and your girl suddenly becomes Halle Berry. Tell me that hasn't happened to you!
5. *Narcissisalgia: It's all about me.* This is the time when you think only about yourself and your own needs.

DIPSTICK: Nice Lip, but mine have actually been scientifically proven. After years and years of research, social scientists have concluded that separateness, coming together, and fusion are healthy components of every relationship.

Unfortunately, many lesbian relationships spend way too much time on number three, either in the throes of being too intimately involved in each other's lives or pining for more. When the merger takes over, you lose sight of yourself. As women, lesbians are natural caregivers and often put their partner's needs before their own. This is not good! That kind of intimacy can overwhelm and smother a person.

Dipstick says for a healthy relationship, you should spend at least one-third of your free time on just you. That's not counting when you're at work. Go to the gym, take a class, write in your room, whatever it is that makes you feel fulfilled and happy. After all, it's those things that made her crazy about you in the first place.

To keep yourself out of dangerous territory, here are ten things Dipstick thinks you should *never* do:

1. Poop when she's in the bathroom. (ick)
2. Always invite her to hang out with your friends.
3. Go somewhere or do something with her that you don't really want to do. (Every once in awhile is OK, but don't make this a habit.)
4. Buy matching outfits.
5. Sell off your Ricky Martin CDs because she doesn't like him.
6. Share underwear.
7. Share a MySpace page.
8. Share a diary.
9. Speak for both of you, saying things like, "We feel . . . We think," etcetera.
10. Buy a bicycle built for two.

Lipstick: Tsk, tsk.

According to Lipstick, these are ten things you should *always* do:

1. Poop when she's in the bathroom if there's a shower curtain between you two. (Be sure to light a match and turn the water on—as long as you're not in an old house. Ouch.)
2. Invite her to happy hour with your cronies. What's the harm in that? Not inviting her is weird.
3. Spend the holidays together, even if it means going to a small town in Texas.
4. Share clothes if you can—imagine how diverse and versatile your wardrobe will be!
5. Get rid of your Ricky Martin CDs. You shouldn't be listening to that garbage anyway.
6. Wash and bleach your underwear, so you can share panties if one of you runs out.
7. Use the Internet without reproach—never have anything in your in-box you wouldn't want your partner to see.
8. Help her design her website if she's design challenged.
9. Forge her signature when necessary on Christmas cards and thank-you notes.
10. Ride your tandem to the wine bar, so you can have a really good time and not drink and drive. You'll have twice as good a chance to get home safely if you're both steering. Be sure to wear helmets!

Codependency

DIPSTICK: Codependency is very common in lesbian relationships. I should know: I once had a codependent girlfriend. At first, it was nice. She always wanted to know how I was feeling and if she could do anything to make me happy. She would get up early to make me coffee and walked my dog when I came home late from work. We never had a problem deciding where to go for dinner, because "Wherever you want" was the choice. The same thing for movies. No arguments ever. It seemed like a match made in heaven. I got to have my cake and eat her, too.

Until the day I decided to go visit my ailing sister. Codependent Rita packed my bag, made me a snack for the drive, and promised to take care of my cat while I was gone. Rita called me every day to see how I was doing and to give me a report on my cat. It was sweet. But when I returned home, I saw immediately that things weren't right. Rita had rearranged all my furniture, waxed my floors, weeded the garden, and mowed the lawn. She filled my fridge with food and had the cat groomed. She went through my address book and called all my friends and told them to send me flowers because I was "having a hard time about my sister." She also called my boss and asked if I could have a light load at work when I got back. I mean, the chick went totally overboard! When I tried to let her know that she didn't need to do all that, she responded with, "Yes, I do. If I don't take care of you, who will?" Granted I had spent many years taking care of myself and my cat too. This time I sent Rita packing. I just couldn't handle all the clinginess.

How do you know if you're dating a codependent? Here are some signs:

- She believes she is the only one who can take care of you.
- She can't make a decision and lets you decide what to do.
- She always seems to need your approval.
- She considers herself to be completely unselfish and dedicated to helping others.
- She has no opinions of her own, yours are good enough.
- She is more loyal than your dog and remains true to you even when you disrespect her.

Lipstick: You're right, Dip, codependency is another one of those hard things to define. It's changed so much since it was established clinically, but essentially, from my own experience, codependency is marked by an unhealthy pattern of living that you've fallen into related to your relationships.

In addition to Dip's signs, here are some others:

- She doesn't believe a word you say, whether it's about where you've been or who you were with. Trust is difficult for her.
- She has to get everything perfect.
- She lacks assertiveness and is unable to communicate her feelings.
- She is ubercontrolling, to the point that she suffocates you.

DIPSTICK: Codependency comes in all shapes and sizes. If you feel like you're codependent or your girlfriend is, get your butts into therapy and figure out how to cut the cord.

But I Paid Last Time

Early finances

"There are people who have money and people who are rich."

—COCO CHANEL

Lipstick: I *love* Chanel—and not only because she makes great fragrances, but because she speaks the damn truth.

Money can be a tricky thing. We need it to survive, but it can kill us, or at the very least kill a good relationship. Like Coco says, it's important to be one of those people who is rich, not money hungry. It's also important to be open and comfortable discussing money.

DIPSTICK: Yeah, but let's face it, Lip, even when you have the right attitude about money, it can still ruin everything, so be careful. Disagreements over finances are the number one problem for couples in America according to a poll from the University of Denver. No matter how little or how much you have, it's bound to be an issue.

Does the butch always pay?

Let's get this out of the way. The butch should not always pay. Just as heterosexual couples are liberating themselves from the man taking control, the femme should feel free to offer to pay at least 50 percent of the time when you are in the early stages of dating. Expecting the butch to always pay is old-fashioned and sexist.

Lipstick: Excuse me for interrupting, but this seems absurd to me. Do some dykes out there really expect the butch to pay?

DIPSTICK: Yes, Lip, and I agree it's absurd, but I've experienced it one too many times.

So, if not along gender lines, how do lesbian couples divide finances?

What happens when she's an Exxon executive and you pump gas

Class differences exist in relationships. They will play out in many ways, but I'll touch on financial ones here. If one of you makes more than the other there are several ways you can handle this. Here are Dipstick's three simple approaches for making money work for you rather than against you:

1. Split things along salary lines. If Kim makes 40 percent more than Justine, then Kim pays 40 percent more of all joint expenses. This includes living and entertainment expenses.
2. Split everything fifty-fifty. If one partner makes much less than the other, then you might have to limit what you do together. No one likes to pay all the time, no matter how rich they are. Certainly it's OK to surprise her with a trip to Hawaii for her birthday from time to time.
3. You can just forget about it all and let it work out as it does. Just pay attention if one of you feels like she's paying more than the other. Then it's time to switch to one of the other plans.

Lipstick: Good financial tips, Charles Schwab.

DIPSTICK: Thanks. Here are some more:

What happens when you feel like you're being taken advantage of?

My friend Kristy is a smart woman. She has her master's degree and runs a nursing unit at a large hospital. When she met Stacy, she was immediately smitten. Stacy was an artist, selling her beautiful jewelry at Gay Pride. Kristy asked Stacy out and before she knew it, they became an item. One day Kristy went to Stacy's place and was appalled at her living conditions. She lived in a rundown apartment on the wrong side of the tracks with little of the natural light she needed for her craft.

Although they had only been dating a few months, Kristy knew she had a big enough house with a garage that Stacy could use for her art. Without giving it too much thought, Kristy asked Stacy to move in. It turns out Stacy didn't make much money from her artwork and what she did make, she used to buy more gold and silver for her craft. Kristy was left paying all the house bills. Resentment eventually built up and Kristy broke up with Stacy. But she couldn't bring herself to ask Stacy to move out. She felt bad about having asked her to give up her apartment. Kristy continued to pay for Stacy's rent, utilities, and food. She was pissed as hell about it, but couldn't make herself kick her out. "She has a dog. I can't stand to see her living in her van," Kristy told me.

In the meantime, Stacy didn't have enough self-respect to move out. She played off Kristy's guilt and generosity. Both women are victims here. Kristy for letting herself get taken advantage of, and Stacy, for not allowing herself to reach her potential of becoming a financially independent woman. If you see yourself in either Kristy or Stacy, make a move now! Get a backbone and take charge of your life.

Lipstick: Don't you think that's a little harsh? Whatever arrangement people have in their relationship is their prerogative.

Here's better advice for all of you power dykes/heiresses out there and the starving artists that Dipstick just pigeonholed:

Be honest. No matter which way you look at it, there's always one person in the relationship with more earning power than the other. Sometimes it's more pronounced than others, but the most important thing about early finances is that you communicate honestly, especially—and absolutely—if you're living together.

When you first meet someone who clearly does better than you financially, don't put on a show. Let her like you for you. Don't let her believe you have a trust fund, or are in another way independently wealthy. You don't have to open your checkbook, but show her by the way you live that you are happy in your life and no matter how little you may bring home at the end of the day, you love what you do (only if that's true, of course). Salaries and vocational fulfillment are almost always tied together, just flipped. Typically, the more you make, the more you dislike the job and the stress it brings. The more you love what you do, the less you make because there are about a million other people who would kill to do what you're doing.

DIPSTICK: That's such BS, Lip. When I was a social worker, I loved my job, but hated that I worked so hard and made so little. It pissed me off that our culture would pay the people who designed soda bottles more than those who were working hard every day to save lives. Being a social worker is a stress-filled job *and* it pays crap. I'm much happier now, making the big bucks as a freelance writer, with much less stress.

Lipstick: So what I said was right—you loved your job and you made peanuts. Regardless of what you make or what your financial arrangements are with your partner, just remember not to let money have immense power over you and your relationship. Try to be smart, but not live in fear, and, like Coco said, be rich!

Are Those My New Shoes?

Boundaries and sharing stuff

Lipstick: When I was in college, I had a housemate named Roseanne who gave new meaning to "no boundaries."

More than once, I came home and found Roseanne wearing my top that was buried somewhere deep in my closet. "Where did you find that?" I asked. She snickered and told me, "Oh, behind your sweaters and piggy bank, zipped up in that suitcase of yours I took to Europe."

Another time, it was my Walkman, which was in my gym bag in my car, hidden underneath snow skis and jumper cables. I tried to talk to her about her lack of boundaries, but mostly I just steamed and gossiped behind her back. Until one day, Rosie went too far.

Roseanne liked to fool around with women. It wasn't common knowledge, but she bragged to me about it, somehow knowing intuitively that I'd like it and wouldn't judge her. One summer night we were drinking a bottle of wine at dinner—just the two of us—and she confessed something that made me hawk my bite of steak into the grass. It was about our other housemate, Jackie, who was always at her boyfriend's house, much to the discontent of Roseanne.

You see, Roseanne had a secret crush on Jackie. It wasn't spoken, but being the budding dyke with wickedly sharp intuition, I knew. I watched Roseanne keep her eyes on Jackie just a hint too long.

"I used Jackie's vibrator last night."

"Holy hell!" I screamed. I couldn't believe she not only had the nerve to do this, but then brag to me about it. Later that night, I installed a lock on my bedroom door and it remained locked until the end of the semester. What if she found my secret stash of old *Curve* magazines? My junior strap-on? I couldn't risk it.

While she never was my lover, her actions made me hypersensitive about boundaries, so when I got into my first relationship, my girlfriend didn't understand why I kept everything locked. "What are you trying to hide?" she asked. It wasn't that I was trying to hide stuff from her, but I was still in armor mode, trying to keep Roseanne's dirty little hands out of my journals and sex toys. I was haunted by her.

Once I shacked up with Texas years later, I was finally able to kick the Brink's security habit, and now I, of course, don't mind sharing anything with her. Whether it's my running shoes or my new Bobbi Brown eyeliner, she can use just about anything of mine.

Texas can't say the same. Even though she's supergenerous in almost all areas of her life, she suffers from only child syndrome, marked by difficulty in sharing things. While I do get her hand-me-down pants when they shrink so much she and her long legs can't wear them, she is fiercely protective of everything else.

DIPSTICK: Only-child syndrome? What the hell is that? I come from a huge family.

Lipstick: Well, let me tell you. It's when you have a hard time sharing stuff because all you ever knew growing up was me, me, me.

DIPSTICK: My experience with Tiger has been quite different. Neither of us is an only child, but we still have had our challenges.

When we first got together, we wore the same type of clothes. It was the early nineties and cutoff Levis, a Michigan T-shirt, and Birkenstocks were the uniform of the day. As a matter of fact, when I first met her, we both laughed at how similar our clothes were. We also happened to be the same size.

When we moved in together, we only had one dresser between us, so all the clothes merged. At first it didn't seem to matter to me who wore the I CAN'T EVEN MARCH STRAIGHT T-shirt or the holey 501 cutoffs. But one day I went to put on my favorite sports bra and I discovered she was wearing it. Suddenly, I flashed back to my childhood. Having been raised an identical twin (yes, there's another Dipstick out there!), Dipstick had to share clothing, and everything else, with her sister. I had flashbacks of screaming at my twin, "Those are my underwear!" while flinging a Partridge Family 45 at her head. Fortunately, I did not have the same reaction with Tiger, even though there was a Tracy Chapman cassette within arm's reach, but at this moment, something became crystal clear: We needed to stop sharing clothing.

The conversation wasn't hard. Once we figured out whose shorts were whose, we bought a secondhand dresser and an amazing thing happened. We each developed our own personal style so different from the other that these days we wouldn't even consider wearing each other's clothes. Slowly she became more feminine and Dipstick moved from androgynous to butch. The more we've differentiated our wardrobes, the more we've grown in other ways as well.

Lipstick: Dip, you used to be a trannie?

DIPSTICK: Sometimes you're so clueless, Lipstick. Being androgynous doesn't mean transsexual.

What to share, what to keep separate

When you move in with your girlfriend, one of the points is to weave your lives together, right? Not so fast. While it's fun to share and mesh your worlds, it's also important to set some boundaries. The trick is, you might not know what your comfort zone is until she mows over it.

This reminds me of a reader who wrote last year. Daria was very excited to move in with Rachael. She carefully unpacked the dishes she inherited from her great-grandmother and placed them gingerly in the curio cabinet. She was appalled the next morning to wake up and find Rachael was using the antique sugar bowl to feed the cat wet food.

Lipstick: Oh, my god! This totally sounds like me and Texas! While our cats have their own darling set of floorware, I believe that dishes should be used, no matter how special. They shouldn't be shoved into a cabinet collecting dust, only to be brought out at the holidays. Texas thinks differently.

DIPSTICK: It never occurred to Daria that Rachael wouldn't treat her prized possessions with the same reverence she did. The couple had their very first fight the morning after they moved in together. Not exactly the honeymoon bliss they expected.

You know what your special items are. Your complete Beatles collection, the jewelry your mother left you, your autographed Sleater-Kinney T-shirt. If there are certain things you treasure, make sure to let your partner know. She won't use that Rolling Stones 1982 concert T-shirt as a dusting rag if she knows the sentimental value. That is, if she respects you. How she treats your stuff can be an indication of how she'll treat your heart. Unless she's like my friend Roxy, who can't hold onto a wine glass to save her soul, even when she's sober. Whenever she comes for a visit I break out the special thrift store glasses I bought with her in mind.

Just remember one thing: it's only stuff. It can be replaced. Can you say the same for the way your new girl warms the bed at night?

Her Dog Chewed My Favorite Belt

Pets

Dear Lipstick and Dipstick,

I just met a really nice lady named Camille and I think we have something special. We have so much in common, we both like Nina Simone and Mary J. Blige. I met her at a spoken word open mic night and she was so sexy and smart. We decided to go on a date and she suggested a walk in the park. "How romantic!" I thought. But then she showed up with her big drooly rottweiler. Turns out, she is crazy about this dog. The problem is I just don't like pets. I mean, I would never hurt an animal or anything, it's just I think they should be kept outside and people inside. It was how I was raised. Is there any hope for us?

Pussy or Her Dog

Lipstick: Are you sure you're a lesbian?

DIPSTICK: Dog Hater, it will never work. Animal freaks should only be with other animal freaks.

Lipstick: For shame, Dipstick. Making sweeping statements is for the birds and you know it. You don't have to be a die-hard animal lover to date someone with pets. When Texas Two-Step and I first got together, I wasn't the biggest cat fan, more of a dog person. But you know what, by the time the first one passed away a few years ago, I was on my knees weeping like a baby, not seeing how I could go on without the Muncy in my life. We've since adopted another cat—Shamus O'Henry—to keep our old Marmalade (who's clinically insane) company. Since the adoption, sometimes I feel like I actually birthed Henry I love him so much. However, I never should have drunk throughout the pregnancy because his eyes are wickedly yellow and he's very hairy.

DIPSTICK: You're the one who's insane, Lip.

What to do when your girl already has a pussy

If you start dating a girl who already has a furry friend, proceed with caution. Be nice to the kitty, but don't dote on her. Take your cues from your partner. Does she treat Felix like a roommate, or does she just throw food on the floor for him once a day? If she treats Princess like her only child, then for God's sake, don't tell her about your stint working in an animal research lab.

If you both have dogs, great! Get them together as soon as possible to make sure they get along, because, if they don't, you're in for some trouble. If it's puppy love at first sight, imagine the beautiful hikes and trips to the doggie bakery and pet-friendly beach resorts.

Lipstick: Texas had our beloved Muncy before we met and I swear that if for some reason she had to pick between me and him back when he was still alive, I'm not sure I would've won. I'm not kidding. I even joked about it once and while she laughed, she didn't reassure me that I wouldn't be the one sent to the shelter.

If your new girlfriend has a pet that she adores, you've got to respect that relationship like you'd respect her if she had a child.

When you want to get a pet together

DIPSTICK: One of the reasons I think Tiger and I have stayed together for so long is that we got a dog two years into our relationship. Once we both fell in love with Juneau, we knew there would be no breaking up. Neither one of us could bear to be without the dog.

So, if you're thinking of getting a pet together, before you do so, evaluate your relationship. How stable are you? If you break up, one of you is going to be doubly heartbroken. I haven't seen the joint custody thing work with animals. They're too used to routine.

Pets are a great way to build your family. Going to your local shelter and saving a kitten in need is a wonderful first step if you're thinking of having children one day. It's a good way to work out the melding of your parenting styles, and like having children, it can strengthen your relationship. After all, Tiger says, "One of the things I love the most about you is how much you love our babies. It makes me love you even more."

The overdoting Chihuahua mom

That said, sometimes lesbians get a little carried away and lavishly love their pets a bit too much. Picture Paris Hilton and her diamond-studded Chihuahua collars. I know lesbians who have had their pit bull's ears pierced and one high femme who actually hennas her standard poodle. At the beginning, this can look sweet and endearing, but beware. Like Lipstick's wife, she might just choose the dog over you one day.

Lipstick: Yep. Take it from me.

When your girl's animal is bad

DIPSTICK: Does Fluffy urinate on your slippers every time you put them under her bed? Is Frisky always trying to get under the covers when you and your honey knock boots? Bad pet behaviors are usually the result of one thing: bad training. Not to say that your new sweetums is neglectful or a bad mom, just that she might need some schooling in proper pet training. The best way to handle this situation is to try to get her to admit her dog needs work and surprise her with a consultation with the hot local dyke dog trainer. Wait, maybe not the hot one, maybe her faithful gay assistant.

Lipstick: I once dated this hottie executive who didn't have time for her dog. She loved him dearly, but was always at the office, leaving little Tango home alone. He would tear her apartment to shreds when she was away and there were enough pee spots on the carpet to think she was going for some sort of polka dot design scheme. When we were home, he would act out and still chew on stuff, looking for attention. The worst part was I lost at least a dozen pair of panties while we were dating. At first, I thought it was the magic vortex in the dryer—you know the one that takes all your socks. Then, one Sunday afternoon, when we were enjoying a nice leisurely stroll through the park with Tango, I had my "aha" moment. Tango had been circling this one tree and got into position. I was waiting with the leash and she with the bag in hand, ready for the pick up, when much to my surprise, I saw my purple paisley panties backing out of Tango's ass. Oh my god! I screamed, pointing at the silk dangling from his doody.

DIPSTICK: Gross, Lip!

Lipstick: I know! Whatever the root of the pet's bad behavior, it's usually telling you something about its owner, so look carefully. In my case, she ended up not having enough time for me either.

The neglectful pet parent

DIPSTICK: We don't like to admit it, but some lesbians just aren't cut out to own pets. Dipstick used to live in an apartment building with a lesbian who, whenever she got a new girlfriend (which was often), she would leave her poor kitty unattended for days, while she and her new catch played cat and mouse at her place. Kitty would climb the curtains, meyowling in such a mournful tone that I couldn't sleep. When I confronted this negligent Nelly about kitty's predicament, she flat out told me the cat was fine as long as it had food and water. Finally I resorted to taking pictures of the distraught animal and posting them on her online dating profile.

Lipstick: You did not!

DIPSTICK: Did, too. I can't say what ever happened to that little animal, because I moved out of the apartment after not too long. A word of caution: If you only learn she has a cat, or worse a dog, after she's spent three nights at your place, she's not relationship material.

I Hate Unloading the Dishwasher!
Chores

DIPSTICK: If there's one thing about chores, it's that you're going to fight about them at one time or another, or regularly. No matter how good a job you think you're doing on keeping the bathroom clean, it's not good enough. Here's what will happen. Your lover will bitch at you for leaving your cereal bowl in the sink. You'll apologize and promise it will never happen again. And then it will happen again. And she'll clean it for you, six or seven more times, until she snaps again.

Chores suck; that's why they're called *chores*. Here are a few ways to deal with the division of labor for those dreaded household tasks.

Make a chart. I know, this reminds you of your shared living arrangements in college, but sometimes it's the only thing that works. Then again, sometimes it doesn't. If Betsy doesn't clean the bathroom one week, then when your turn comes up on the wheel, it will be extra disgusting and you'll throw a fit. Trust me, I know.

Don't make a chart. Tiger and I have worked out a system that works pretty well. We only fight an average of once a month about chores, so I think it's mostly successful. We've split up the chores. I take out the garbage, vacuum, mow the lawn, change the oil, cook, clean the bathroom, dust, make the bed, clean the litter box and the windows. She fills the ice cube trays. I hate filling the ice cube trays.

Lipstick: Dip, will you talk to Lonestar about how your chores are split up? Even though she's femme, I want her to be the butch when it comes to chores. I can handle the ice trays.

DIPSTICK: All right Lip, I'll talk to her, but just keep one thing in mind: She's not your maid. But maybe you can dress her up and pretend? Think of it: You'll get turned on and the house will get cleaned all at the same time!

Lipstick: Now you're talking! Here are some more things you can do, ladies:

Have sex instead of chores. Throw that damn toilet scrubber out the window and grab your dildo instead! That'll pacify the angst surrounding the dirty house. Once your honey has an orgasm, she'll forget all about that cereal bowl in the kitchen sink.

Hire a maid. And a hot one, too. It's probably best if she's straight, so the lusting is innocent.

DIPSTICK: I prefer gay male house cleaners. They really get in between the cracks.

Lipstick:

Have more sex. Duh. When you feel the anger starting to swell again, have a new sex toy waiting in the wings. If her anger is about the four-foot-high pile of laundry, throw her on the washer, put it on the spin cycle, and show her how the Rabbit Habit works.

Then Comes the Baby Carriage

Having babies

Babies. Oh babies. They have broken up more relationships than the bad girl at the bar. The reasons these little puke heads have destroyed many fruitful unions are myriad—they range from one partner deciding there's not a maternal bone in her body, to not wanting the responsibility, to the baby killing your sex life. It's a very big decision and one that shouldn't be made without much thought, discussion, and processing.

Are you ready to start a family?

1. Poop
   a. Love it!
   b. Hate it!
   c. Whatever!

2. Throw up
   a. Love it!
   b. Hate it!
   c. Whatever!

3. Sleep
   a. Hate it!
   b. Love it!
   c. Whatever!

4. Snotty noses
   a. Love them!
   b. Hate them!
   c. Whatever!

5. Social life
   a. Not important.
   b. Very important.
   c. Whatever.

If you answered "a" to most of these questions

DIPSTICK: Sorry, you won't make a good parent. You're deluding yourself. You think giving up your life and yourself is what it takes to be a parent. Sorry, honey, you're wrong. Parents need to be strong people with realistic heads on their shoulders.

Lipstick: Your child may end up on *America's Most Wanted* if you're not careful.

If you answered "b" to most of these questions

DIPSTICK: You'll make a good parent. You're realistic about the downside of parenting and you're going into this with eyes wide open.

Lipstick: Your child will grow up to be a great, levelheaded person and will be there to hold your hand when you have that nervous breakdown at forty.

If you answered "c" to most of these questions

DIPSTICK: Congratulations, you'll make an excellent parent. You got that go-with-the-flow personality and flexibility that is exactly what's missing from most controlling dyke moms.

Lipstick: Oh, dear dyke, you are going to be the PTA Mother of the Year and your child will be a straight-A student and a stellar concert pianist. You'll raise her well and she'll go through life with her head high, fighting for our rights as a straight ally.

DIPSTICK: Beyond our quiz, we're not going to get into the how to's of having a baby. There are plenty of books that will help you with that. We're not going to help you figure out if you should inseminate or adopt, as there are pros and cons to each. What we're concerned about right now is saving your relationship during the whole baby process.

Here are some questions/snags we hear about from mothers out there in the field:

What happened to our love life?

There's nothing like 3:00 A.M. feedings, poopy pants, and screaming ear infections to put you in the mood for hot sex. And on the off chance that you peel yourself away from Johnny Jr. long enough to feel a little frisky and you go looking for your lover, you'll find her asleep.

Lipstick: Dipstick, you've got to be the most pessimistic person I know.

DIPSTICK: I'm getting to the positive spin, so hold your horses. Sex when there's a newborn in the house will definitely slack off, but it's up to you to keep the romantic fire stoked as the baby grows to toddle and heads off to school. It's very important for your relationship to make couple time. I can't emphasize this enough. At least once a month, you need to make a date for intimacy. Get your sister to watch the kids, go out to dinner, a movie, or rent a hotel room downtown. We don't care what it is, as long as it's just you and your girlfriend. Two rules:

1. You can't talk about the kids.
2. You must have sex.

Lipstick: Why does the intimacy have to wane when you get prego or have a baby? I understand that life gets hectic when you have a baby, but I think people go into the baby business with those expectations (which function, ultimately, as intentions) and then it's a self-fulfilling prophecy. To me, I think that having a little mugwump would only enhance intimacy between two partners, looking at the little jewel they've created. During this time, when the mothers might be tired and drained from getting up to change a poopy diaper, maybe the best thing to do is to focus on masturbating together. It's easy and quick and continues bonding the women sexually.

DIPSTICK: But please wash your hands after diaper duty!

Can you help? I can't get pregnant

Getting pregnant is harder than you think. Especially for those of us who can't shoot sperm from our dildos. For lesbians, the process of getting pregnant can be very expensive, medically invasive, and just plain weird. I mean, you get this big tanker filled with dry ice delivered to your house. You trek it to the doctor's office, where she extracts the sperm with a syringe and inserts it into your vagina. If you're lucky, your partner is there, holding your hand. Even if she is, the sterile doctor's office isn't the most romantic environment.

When the pregnancy process takes months or years, it can wreak havoc on your relationship. All kinds of irrational emotions that you swore you would never have come up. You can't stand to be around other lesbians with babies. You fall into a deep depression every time you get your period. All you can think and talk about is how much you want/need to have a baby.

While all of these feelings are real, they can be a monster to be around. Get yourself into a support group for other mothers who can't conceive.

I want to have kids, but my partner doesn't—what should I do?

Lipstick: This is a tough one. You can't infuse the motherly instinct into a woman, especially a dyke who's resolved that she's not having kids. If you find yourself in this stalemate, what you first need to do is talk, talk, and then talk some more. Then, once you begin beating a dead horse, go see a therapist.

If you're one of those women who really wants kids, you're probably not going to change your mind. If you do, and you're weak enough that your partner is able to convince you otherwise—even though deep down you know it's what you want—then you're going to end up resenting her and being really sorry. You didn't follow your gut. Once your window of fertility slams shut, it's closed for good.

Then there's the one who does want kids. Manipulating or forcing her to have a child is the worst thing you could do. Yet, it can be so tricky because you love her and the life you've created together so much. In the end, Lipstick believes that even though you adore your girlfriend and your relationship, your intuitive tug to have kids is something you shouldn't ignore. You must honor that ticking biological clock.

I can't stress the need to see a therapist enough. Don't just wait until you're ready to start looking for donors to start dealing either; start early to give you both time to process sans the pressure of the sperm arriving at your front door.

Don't be discouraged if your girl doesn't think she wants kids. I think a lot of parents go into parenthood fearful, doubtful, and unsure what to expect. Just be honest, communicate well, and follow your instincts. Life always unfolds as it should. Trust that.

Opening the Floodgates

Later finances

Shared bank accounts

DIPSTICK: To joint or not to joint? Dipstick strongly advises against merging finances too quickly. Tiger and I didn't get a joint account until we bought a house together. It's not that I didn't trust her; it's just that she never balanced her checkbook and I liked how my numbers came out all nice and even at the end of each month. Unless there is a reason to go joint with your expenses, don't do it.

Lipstick: If you're in an LTR with someone, a woman you see yourself growing old with, why not share a bank account? It's only money and it simplifies things. No more "You pay for this" and "I'll pay for that." How tiring. If you're living together, and most certainly if you own a home together, get a joint checking account. If you've got a massive savings or a trust fund, then keep a separate account for your little nest egg and dip into it as you see fit. Otherwise, I highly encourage you to keep a joint primary checking account that you use for bills, mortgages, a new furnace, dinners out, trips, etcetera.

There may be challenges in commingling money, but once you work through them, you'll be glad you did it. Besides, working through financial trials will only strengthen your relationship. Here are some of the challenges you may face:

Different banking habits. One of you never writes her charges in the checkbook and this causes the other much distress because the checkbook doesn't balance. This has been somewhat curbed since the invention of online banking, since you can see your charges as you make them online (note to self: Big Brother is watching).

Different spending habits. One of you is a penny pincher, the other is a spendthrift. This one hits close to home. You see, Lipstick is a spender. (Probably not a big surprise.) I'm impulsive and generous and believe money should be spent, constantly ebbing and flowing in and out of one's account. This is challenging to Texas, God bless her Lonestar soul, because, although she loves to shop, she can't do nearly the damage I can without blinking an eye. Even if we had all the money in the world, she would still have two bags at the end of the day and I would have two rented mules to carry my stuff. I'm all about abundance in every area of my life.

DIPSTICK: That's why I took away your Lipstick & Dipstick credit card . . .

Different math skill sets.

Lipstick: This one also hits me right in the wallet. I hate math; I don't mind adding, subtracting, dividing, and multiplying (I even won a flashcard contest in seventh grade. Go, little Lipstick). Ask me what six tubes of Smashbox lip gloss cost and *boom*: I've got your answer. Wanna know how much a dozen new champagne flutes will set you back? Done. But don't you dare ask me to balance the checkbook, because I'll suddenly come down with a fever.

In the beginning of our relationship, I made Téjas a deal: I'll stick with rug munching if she did the number crunching. Seems I got the sweet end of the deal because she really does both. Either way, I don't think she'd mind because she genuinely gets off on balancing the checkbook and paying bills online. She shouts in pure ecstasy when the numbers match. "Yes!" she screams from the office. I, on the other hand, would rather be working with sweaty men laying fresh asphalt on a hot Arizona day than balancing that damn register.

Tightwad versus the wad blower.

DIPSTICK: Money, like jealousy, can poison any relationship. When both of you have different spending habits, not only will it cause fights, it may cause you to break up. This is serious shit, so listen up!

When she has bad credit. Can you all believe that the average household has thirteen credit cards, and the average American carries nearly $6,000 in credit card debt? Those monthly payments can add up, and if you're not careful, you can get in over your head. And then you know what happens . . . you're late on your car payment (ding on credit), or you can't quite pay the phone bill because you just started dating that long-distance lover you met online. Ding, ding, ding. The dings add up and equal bad credit. If she has bad credit and you're worried about her spending or sharing a bank account, you should be: bad credit can take years to repair, so don't get into any financial deals with her until she gets her credit score up. Don't move in with her, don't cosign on her car loan, and for princess sake, don't cosign on a credit card for her! Bad credit isn't necessarily a clear veto on a relationship, but it is a big warning sign. What's more important is her attitude about it. Is she actively working to repair her credit, or is she running it up and up and up?

Lipstick: Why are you picking on poor souls who have let a few credit cards get out of hand?

DIPSTICK: I'm not picking on anyone. I'm just trying to warn women about getting involved with someone who has financial problems. It suggests other problems. Even though I understand that because the national minimum wage is poverty level, it's hard for people to make ends meet, and credit cards can sometimes help you get over that hump, Americans need to learn to live within their means. Come to think of it, it sounds like a governmental conspiracy. The credit card companies and the lawmakers are in bed together!

It's not about trust. Sure, you may be head over heels in love. You may be thinking the two of you are going to spend the rest of your lives together, but look at your life goals. Where do you see yourself in ten years? Wouldn't it suck if she's not in the picture, but you're left with a payment, month after month, with nothing to show for it but a bleeding heart, some worthless eBay crap, and a bad credit report? Trust has nothing to do with it.

Cosigning a loan. Never cosign a loan with a term longer than you've been together. Actually scratch that. Don't get a loan at all, pay cash. The only two things you should go into debt for are your house and your education.

Lipstick: Or the half-yearly sale at Nordstrom's.

DIPSTICK: If you can't afford to pay cash for a new car, get a used one. Set up a bank account that you make "car" payments into. You'll be earning the interest rather than giving it away to a bank. In the meantime, ride your bike. It's better for the environment and your health.

Credit cards. There are two days Dipstick remembers fondly as the freest days of my life. The first was when I came out of the closet, the second was the day I paid my last credit card bill and cut them all up. I keep one around for emergencies and car rentals. Other than that, credit cards are just bad news. If you can't pay cash for it, don't do it.

Sure that vacation to Tahiti sounds great, but won't you appreciate it more if you save until you have enough to pay cash for it? And don't get in the trap of buying her expensive gifts. There are so many ways to show her love that don't involve money.

Lipstick: But, every femme knows that true love comes in a little blue box.

DIPSTICK: You can see why Lipstick and I are not in a relationship.

The worst thing you can go into debt over is eating out at expensive restaurants. By the time the credit car bill comes due, you won't even remember what you ate. By the time it's paid off, you'll have gained and lost that five pounds seven times.

Lipstick: Boy, Dipstick, we are like yin and yang when it comes to how to handle finances. Good thing we aren't married—I'd see the big D in our future.

There's nothing wrong with credit—extending yourself a little further—if used wisely. After all, most small businesses (ours included) started out on plastic. Plastic can give means to a dream.

Not only can a little plastic help make dreams come true, it's a great alternative to use when shopping and out to dinner—as long as you pay it off right away. You can earn miles and not have to worry about marking it in that silly register.

I do agree with Dipstick that you should exercise some caution when entering into a financial obligation with a girl who has excessive debt, especially if she's ambivalent about it. Even though those damn credit card companies make a boatload of dough on us frivolous Americans, it's still someone else's money you're borrowing and should be paid back as soon as possible; however, I don't think you should judge people and their financial problems in such a heartless way. Be careful, but don't be narrow-minded.

Putting her through college.

DIPSTICK: When Tiger finally decided to quit her barista job and head back to school to pursue her lifelong goal of becoming a graphic designer, I was elated. I imagined dropping her off at the bus stop in her cute school-girl skirt and tight sweater, a stack of books hugged tightly to her chest. She'd come home with chalk smudged on her fingers and we'd sneak a few kisses in before she sat down to do her homework, while I monitored, ruler in hand.

Although she did finish school with honors and awards, my fantasies didn't exactly come true. The fact is, while I knew she was going to college to better our lives, the temporary financial burden was challenging. While I was working and bringing home the same amount of money as always, she suddenly had to spend what little she had saved on poster board and expensive computer programs. Even if we did have the money to go out to dinner or see plays, she didn't have the time. Luckily, I had my riding club and volunteer stint at the community radio station to keep me busy while she toiled away at the library.

I didn't put my wife through school. I couldn't have afforded it if I wanted to. She took out loans that we are still paying back. If your expenses are intertwined, you'll both end up taking the burden of one of you returning to school. If one of you is paying the way for the other, this is a good time to get some things in writing.

There is no guarantee what will happen in the next four years. Your lady is out, learning new things and growing in different ways. Although you both may look at her going to school as an investment in your future together and neither of you might want to admit it, these changes may mean she decides to move on from the relationship. It's just a good idea to be clear about finances before you take out a second mortgage on your house to set her up with a supply of shiny new pencils. If you're really worried, you can even get each of your intentions in writing and have them notarized.

Lipstick: Dip, good lord. Why do you have to make everything some big, grim, issue-filled ordeal? Yes, having one person in school does have its financial challenges—I, too, went back to school when Téjas and I first got together—but just because your girlfriend wants a bachelor's degree doesn't mean she wants to be a bachelorette. Texas never brought me a contract saying I wouldn't leave her, even when my creative writing degree helped me become a big advice columnist, and it's a good thing, because I would've been appalled if she had. If you think you need to get things in writing about her chasing after a dream for the betterment of both your lives, I wonder if you should even be together.

DIPSTICK: The contract is not a guarantee you won't leave her, but a plan to pay the money back you borrow. Whether it's in writing or not, a plan is a good idea.

Lipstick: Nope, go with the flow.

Homo Sweet Homo

Buying a house

DIPSTICK: When Tiger and I decided it was time to buy a house, I thought that's simply what we were doing—buying a house. Boy was I wrong. The house was such a small part of it.

Right away, all of our issues came to the surface and we had to learn to speak up about what was really important to us and compromise on things that weren't.

Before you buy a house, no doubt each of you will make a list of everything you want. What neighborhood you want to be in, size of the yard, fireplace or not, garage, how many bedrooms, and so on. Your lists may or may not mesh.

For example, a porch was really important to me. There's nothing Dipstick loves more than sitting out in the morning breeze with her coffee watching the neighbors scurry off to work from the comfort of her front porch. Tiger didn't care about a porch; she wanted a fenced yard for the dog. As a matter of fact, that was top on her list. We could have been in the worst neighborhood in town, in a tiny one-bedroom craphole, as long as there was a big yard for the dog. Needless to say, we had our first argument when we came upon a house in a good neighborhood, with no character, no curb appeal, and a terrible layout. But it had a great backyard for a dog. She wanted to put in an offer right away. I wasn't so sure. Chances were, we'd be living in this house long after our dog was dead and buried.

You'd better hope your relationship is solid, because buying a house together will challenge it. Even if it's been smooth sailing leading up to it, prepare for the shit to hit the fan.

Buying a house is about asking for what you want. It's about listening to what she wants. It's about learning how you each deal with money. It's about understanding how to compromise. It's about living within your means. It's about getting out of your fantasy and facing reality.

Everything is under the roof

Buying a house brings it all up. Expect to deal with all these issues and more. In addition to the money issues, expect to face self-esteem challenges, communication roadblocks, and relationship dynamics. Hell, we could write a whole book on this, couldn't we, Lipstick? Perhaps Texas, the realtor, would like to help us write it?

Before you buy a house

DIPSTICK: No one wants to talk about a potential break up when they're making a big commitment like buying a house together, but Dipstick recommends coming up with a plan. That's right, a prenup that spells everything out. If you break up, what will happen with the house? Will one of you buy the other out? If so, at what price? Current market value or based on what is owed on the loan? What about the furniture? Is one of you going to put more money into the house than the other? How will you deal with that if you split?

Lipstick: There you go again. I'm surprised you didn't make me sign one as your irreverent cohort.

DIPSTICK: Lip, here's why I'm so big on the plans: My friend Aubrey fell in love with a hot contractor named Alix. Alix had a bod to die for from all her years of pounding nails and carrying boards around. Aubrey couldn't help herself and soon Alix moved into her house. After two years together, Alix wanted her own shop. She didn't have much money, but Aubrey did, so she sold her old house and bought a larger one with a nice shop in back. Alix promptly went to work fixing it up and soon it was their dream home. Problem was it wasn't their dream relationship. After a year of living in the new place, Alix and Aubrey broke up. On paper, Aubrey owned the house and all its equity, but Alix had put her sweat and carpentry talent into the home. Two lawyers and a nasty settlement later, Aubrey wished she had spelled everything out in the beginning. Don't let yourself fall into this scenario. Like I said, get a prenup and have a lawyer or notary sign it.

Lipstick: Oh geez. This is about as sexy as pulling out a sheet of dental dam when you first go down on your girlfriend.

DIPSTICK: You might not find it sexy, but like the latex, it's necessary protection.

Lipstick: Unless there's a lot of money at stake—hundreds of thousands— deciding who's going to buy who out in the event you break up is a lousy way to start your first home together. Plus, it takes all the fun out of it. Don't take Dipstick's advice, ladies. It will set you up for failure. Sure, I don't live in a fantasy world; I realize that sometimes even perfect relationships can break down and crumble to pieces if not properly cared for, but a prenup? If you think having a prenup is a good idea, perhaps you should set up an LLC for your relationship, too, so neither of you is liable for damages when you drive the car through the front porch after you find out she's cheated on you. Or why not incorporate the union and have your friends be on the board of directors. All those in favor of sending Lipstick and Texas on a two-week vacation to the Halekulani in Waikiki this summer say "aye."

DIPSTICK: Hey Lip, that's a great idea. If we can't have marriage rights, maybe we can get corporation benefits.

Lipstick: I do agree with Dipstick on one thing: If one partner puts $100,000 (or whatever) down on the home and the other nothing, it should be crystal clear that if there's a breakup or a buyout or a sell off, then she's entitled to her initial cash back, including whatever equity split is decided upon at the termination. If you've been together longer than three years, I believe everything else should be split down the middle.

Buying a house isn't brain surgery or a nasty mediation, it's a blessed event

As usual, Dipstick is all doom and gloom on this subject—arguments over porches and fenced-in yards, prenups, and carpentry. Buying a house with your girlfriend is a big deal (especially your first) and should be nothing but joyful. Sure, there are lots of things to consider and plenty of compromising, but that's all in a day's work in a relationship. She wants sushi, you want steak—so you end up at Benihana. Instead of compromising over mayo and Miracle Whip, it's a garage or a finished basement. By the time you actually move in together, you should be old pros when it comes to compromising. After the good ole Triple P—which you all went through, right?—buying a house should be a cinch. As with most things in life, it's all about the approach.

Full sun or shade garden

I'm a full sun kind of girl—I see the bright side of things, dream big, and believe there's still goodness in the world. I like to grow tomatoes and wild ideas, both of which require a lot of Vitamin D and positive thinking.

Much like Dip, Texas is a bit of a shade gardener, so it can sometimes be challenging to find a garden that we're both happy with. Since the Southern Belle and I started dating many years ago, I've learned a lot about compromise and realize that so much of a successful union is—aside from sexual chemistry and similar interests—finding that common ground, that garden with both shade and sun.

This translates to every other area of our life, too. When I find myself being a stickler about what I want, I have to stop, remind myself that we're in a relationship, one which I entered into blissfully, and we must figure out what we want together. I've learned the hard way that it's not just about me, and no matter how much I'd like to think I've got all the answers, she's right sometimes and her desires are just as important as my own. Keep this in mind when you're looking for a house; remember you both have to live there and depending what's on the market, you'll have to be flexible with your wish list. Bend, bitches!

Country Club versus Double-Wide
Dealing with differences

We deal with differences in our relationships all the time. She likes Thai food and you're into Indian. She likes to jog and you're a sprinter. She likes to read and you watch TV. Some differences are bigger, more ingrained. Have no fear, fellow dykes; seemingly insurmountable differences can be overcome with a little patience and guidance from Lipstick & Dipstick.

Vegetarian versus meat eater

Lipstick: Because so many lesbos love animals and are at one point or another moved to tears over the harmful treatment of animals, vegetarians are very common in the dyke community. Even though we're softies when it comes to fauna—and are usually on a strict fish diet in other areas of life—many of us still enjoy a juicy steak or a big rotisserie chicken dripping with sweat and Italian seasonings.

A vegetarian and a meat eater typically don't run into snags if they both respect the other and don't proselytize about their eating habits. This statement isn't true when it comes to the grill, as I've seen cat fights erupt between lovers whose chicken skewers and tofu patties were touching on the old Webster. In their defense, these spats are usually isolated to hot summer days when we're all a little crabby and need another ice cold Corona. Make a habit of keeping your lamb shank away from her Tofurky and you should be fine.

DIPSTICK: When we first hooked up, Tiger was a strict vegetarian, which didn't bother me at all. Even though I do love me some bacon and a beefy burger, I do cook mean marinated tofu and vegetarian chili, so things went along great for a while. I'll tell you what happened as the years went by. Tiger became more and more curious about my shrimp curry and would sneak "just a taste."

The next thing I knew, she was whipping up her own turkey burgers and tuna casseroles. We're not unique either; I've seen this in the meat/no meat relationship time and time again. The veg is usually a carnivore by year five, even if it's "only on Thanksgiving." Trust Dipstick on this one.

Clean and sober versus boozehound

Lipstick: This can be tricky (or rather tipsy) business. From my pool of experience, it seems that a boozer and someone in recovery from alcoholism can still have a great relationship if—and this is a big if—the one going to AA has been sober for many years. A seasoned sober-ite can handle the alcohol smell on her girlfriend's breath when they kiss good night and not feel her sobriety is jeopardized by the six-pack of Hefeweizen in the fridge.

DIPSTICK: I totally disagree, Lipstick. Boozers and gals in recovery rarely make it. Sooner or later that gin kiss is going to trigger Ms. AA. She's going to feel you're "not present" and "using alcohol to numb your feelings." Her clean and sober friends are going to get on her case for dating a drinker and warning her about the danger of relapse.

Sober girls, you know the drill—don't date anyone unless you both have a year of sobriety under your belts. Drinkers, don't go trolling AA meetings for a date, but if you do meet a hot addict, enroll yourself in Al-Anon pronto.

Tennis camp versus fresh air child

Lipstick: Coming from two different backgrounds can be a bigger challenge than you'd think. Being raised in a household where you had to watch your parent's struggle to pay bills puts a different skin on you, much different than that supple dermis of the girl who never had to go through tough times, the princess who had the trampoline and the horse she dreamed about, the one who got the car of her choice at sixteen when you had to ride the city bus.

I have a theory: Lesbians of different classes never make it into a long-term relationship; they fizzle out before the relationship even gets started because how we were raised is ingrained into everything. The way we talk, the things we like to do, how we travel, where we go, where we like to eat, how we decorate, etcetera. You name it, it's a byproduct of the soil we grew up in.

DIPSTICK: I think class differences show up on the first date. How much tip you leave, how you dress for dinner, even which restaurant you go to can all be traced back to what class you come from. Even if you both earn about the same, the amount of money your parents made and their attitude about money can impact your relationships today. But that doesn't mean you can't make it work.

Julie and Marie are a great example. Julie comes from a poor family. Her single mom struggled to keep food on the table for her and her two sisters. Once, when her mom lost her job, they were forced to live in their car for a few months. Marie, on the other hand, grew up with middle-class parents. She was taught that if she did all the right things—went to college and got a good job—she would be well provided for. She saw her dad go off to work each day at his business, while her mom stayed at home and cooked meals for her and her brother, volunteered at her school, and played golf with her friends. Julie saw her mother break her back, working as a waitress in a diner and cleaning other people's houses. To Julie, hard work did not get you ahead; it only made you tired and cranky. Even though Julie was able to go to college on student loans and has a well-paying job, she still struggles to pay off her loans and send money to her mom every month. Marie, on the other hand, calls her family weekly to hear about the trips they have planned to the Caribbean and Europe.

Coming from backgrounds as diverse as this, Julie and Marie are going to run into issues from the get-go. Marie wishes Julie would take out a loan and buy herself a new car and Julie squirms when Marie sends her burger back because it is too well done.

The big thing about class differences in America is that we don't acknowledge they exist. Because they both went to college and work in the same field, Marie does not think of Julie as coming from another class, but how we are raised to think and act around money and material things can have a lifelong impact on our worldview, our self-esteem, and our thoughts about the future. If a couple like Marie and Julie want to make it, they'll both have to educate themselves about class differences.

When Dipstick was a social worker she attended a workshop where everyone was lined up in a big room. People were told to take a step forward for privileges such as parents went to college, grandparents owned a business, or parents owned a home. Others had to take a step backward for oppressions like having been homeless, incarcerated, or coming from a nonwhite family. This exercise clearly demonstrated that contrary to how most Americans see it, we're not all on an equal playing field. Those who come from backgrounds with lots of oppression have much to overcome, just to get to the starting line.

For couples who come from different class or cultural backgrounds, an exercise like this can be a good starting point to discuss how their backgrounds affect their current life outlook. If couples aren't able to talk about and deal with these differences, their relationship has little chance of success.

Buddhist versus Catholic guilt

Lipstick: I dated a Catholic girl once and let me tell you, she was smokin' hot! We fell wildly in love very quickly and things were great . . . for the first few months. Then gradually, like a cold you can't get rid of, her Catholic guilt began crawling into our relationship. It started slowly at first, so slowly in fact, I didn't notice right away. After sex, as we were lying in each other's arms, I started noticing she wasn't falling asleep right away—she just stared at the ceiling with this dull malaise.

The end finally came when her grandmother died. From that moment on, she was too paralyzed with fear that Grannie was watching from heaven to engage in the bedroom. Those of you who aren't religious might be shaking your head, saying "No way." But trust me here, ladies, it's the truth. Her Vatican-induced fear was very real.

There can be a big gap between two people who believe different dogmas, no matter who they worship or what they believe. As with many organized religions, the Catholic way of life has a crippling side effect, one loaded with (no offense to all your Catholics out there—I'm generalizing here based on observation) guilt, shame, and inflexible obligation.

DIPSTICK: Lipstick, you'd better stop before you end up forced on your knees and gagged with rosary beads.

Lipstick: I might like that.

DIPSTICK: Dipstick was raised Catholic and I can be the first to attest that we have no more guilt about being gay than say, the Jews or Southern Baptists. As a matter of fact, we Catholics have so much symbolism to draw from that our sexual fantasies are full blown.

Forget Madonna and her priest fetish—think confessionals, Catholic schoolgirl outfits, and my favorite: the all-woman sanctuary known as the convent. Where do you think we got the idea of women-only events?

Peace activist versus colonel

Lipstick: What happens when you take time out of your busy "Code Pink: Women for Peace" protests to go to a friend's housewarming party and meet the love of your life . . . only to find out AFTER you smooch and you're fully smitten that she's a retired army colonel with a purple heart?

This combo rarely ever happens because what fundamentally makes someone either a peace activist or a military girl are too far askew. Still, sometimes who we fall for is out of our control—our libido is in control, the only honest gauge. You may not agree with each other (When I first started dating Texas, she was a Republican! She's since wised up.). If you're in this boat, don't worry, it doesn't mean that you're going to drown. There are things you can do besides bailing. (Unless the colonel voted for Bush the second time and still stands by that vote, then you should get the f— out!)

How can two people with such inherent differences make it work?

One word: RESPECT. Respect. Respect. Respect.

DIPSTICK: That's one word, but why do you have to say it four times? I've got to say, all those years hanging out at military bases, protesting the war, it was bound to happen. A cute Air Force MP threw her plastic handcuffs on me as I chanted with my sisters, "Peace now! No more war victims!" I swear her brush against my bosom was intentional . . . and I liked it!

Sure enough, when I was released later and given my trespassing ticket, who was waiting outside the base, this time in street clothes, offering to drive me back to the peace camp in her red Camaro? That's right, Ms. MP.

The sexual tension was thick. To this day, I regret turning down her proposition.

Lipstick: You pussy.

DIPSTICK: I know. While I was thinking, "This will never work: a military cop and a peace activist," I shouldn't have been so long sighted. We probably could've had a wonderful night of making love not war.

That said, unless your military gal is retired, a relationship with someone in the armed forces is risky. (If Don't Ask, Don't Tell is repealed by the time this book is published, then ignore this advice.) Being with someone in the closet will kill you, not quickly like a nuclear bomb blast, but slowly, like the radiation that will eat you from the inside out.

Butch versus femme

Lipstick: Were Dipstick and I meant to write about this, or what? Butch and femme women go together like peanut butter and jelly, like Thelma & Louise, like . . . Lipstick & Dipstick! Not too many problems arise when a butch and a femme are together. In fact, many problems arise when there isn't a butch/femme dynamic.

DIPSTICK: Lipstick, what would you know about the butch/femme dynamic? So far as I can see, you haven't dated any butches.

Lipstick: No, I dated a Dipstick once. She was quite a lover, too.

DIPSTICK: Oh, probably because you didn't have to do any of the work.

Lipstick: What do you mean by that? I made breakfast.

DIPSTICK: Here's the thing about butch/femme. It's not so much how you identify to the outside world, but how you relate as a couple. I think in every relationship, a butch/femme dynamic exists, whether you admit it or not.

Lipstick: Oh, that's bullshit. Texas and I are both femmes.

Lipstick's Fashion Tips for Couples

Don't Match

Never wear matching clothing items, even if someone has a gun to your head. This is especially important when it comes to items with patterns. Variants of the same pattern are also a big homo no-no.

This happens by chance sometimes with Texas and me. I'll leave early for Lipstick & Dipstick Headquarters and kiss her good-bye while she's still hitting the snooze button. Then we'll meet for dinner somewhere and we'll gasp when we first realize we have on matching outfits. The solution: get takeout.

So remember, don't wear matching prints or matching coats or matching anything on the same day, even if you're on a Royal Caribbean cruise or at a family reunion. There are no exceptions. If you want people to know you're together, hold hands.

Don't Criticize

If you don't like your partner's style, don't criticize her. Unless she doesn't have any style at all—then it's all right to do something drastic, but

DIPSTICK: Right. When's the last time your wife wore a skirt?

Lipstick: 1994.

DIPSTICK: Exactly. If you have an open mind and look at your relationship, you'll see that one of you naturally takes on a more masculine role. Look at Bette and Tina from *The L Word*. Most people will say they're both femmes, but 99 percent of the time, if you ask fellow dykes who is the butch, they'll say Bette.

Lipstick: Where are you going with this, Dipstick? They're not even real people; they're TV characters.

DIPSTICK: All I'm trying to say is that butch/femme is a natural way for lesbians to relate to one another. That said, there are no prescribed ways to be butch/femme. Being butch doesn't mean you have to wear flannels and be careful. Years ago, Texas's Melissa Etheridge 1990 T-shirt nearly caught the house on fire.

Do Borrow

If you're lucky enough to be the same size and the same style, have at it! You'll have twice the wardrobe if you share clothes with your partner. It's important to note that, while this can fantastically expand your wardrobe, it can also cause some nasty fights.

Do Compliment Each Other

If she looks hot, tell her and tell her often. Women can't hear enough how attractive they are.

Other Fashion Faux Pas

Christmas sweaters. Box them up and send them to the North Pole! This goes for hairdos, too—avoid the same hairstyle at all costs. Even though it's our tendency to merge, enmeshment is not a pretty fashion statement.

drive a Harley and I know plenty of gorgeous femmes who never wear makeup. But the butch/femme dynamic is real and the chemistry undeniable. When in a relationship together, butches and femmes have a few things to keep in mind.

For Lipsticks

- She may not pick up her boxers from the floor, but she takes good care of your car.
- She may leave a mess in the kitchen, but at least she cooks.
- 501s *are* dress pants.

For Dipsticks

- If femmes weren't high maintenance, you wouldn't love them.
- Yes, she really does need to change three times before you go out.

- Listen to them when they tell you what to wear; it's more important they like how you look and they know best about fashion.

Interracial relationships

DIPSTICK: After my friend Shaunisha ended her last relationship, she swore she would never date a white woman again. Then she met Tina. Shaunisha was drunk, so all she noticed was how Tina knew all the words to the R & B songs she sang growing up and could move like Beyoncé on the dance floor. She didn't notice Tina was white, and sometimes she still forgets. And according to Shaunisha, that's what makes their relationship work.

Cultural differences don't have to be a big deal in a relationship, unless you make it a big deal. Each of you needs to be open to seeing things from the other person's point of view. What is critical is what's important in any relationship: sharing common values, enjoying the same things, and sexual compatibility.

However, couples in cross-cultural relationships still have to deal with the outside world, which can be racist and harsh. Issues of race and privilege may come up when one of you is treated unfairly. For example, a friend of mine complained to her white girlfriend that she was treated rudely by a store clerk and she was sure it was because she is black. Her girlfriend thought she was being too sensitive and said the guy was probably having a hard day, but she was willing to hear her partner out and because of it, came to understand how the two of them see the world differently because of their cultural experiences.

Another friend of mine said, "I constantly forget that I am in an interracial relationship. For me, for us, it is an absolute nonissue. I firmly believe that racial and culture differences have very little to do with personal relationships and people's ability to get along or not. In any relationship, communication and understanding/open-mindedness are essential. I would suggest those as ways to 'make it work' with anyone."

Robbing the cradle

DIPSTICK: No one is better qualified to answer this section than Lipstick.

Lipstick: Damn right. Texas is ten years older than me and I love it.

Growing up, I wasn't always attracted to older women. It's not a pattern for me and looking back, I've never dated anyone who was more than a year older. But, oh how I fell for Texas. When we met, age didn't matter. Our connection was organic. It didn't matter that when I was learning my ABCs, she was moving into her freshman dorm. It didn't matter that when I first got my period she was getting her first job out of college. None of these things mattered and they still don't.

Sure, when Texas and I first started dating, it was very much an issue . . . for everyone else. Her friends said it wouldn't work, that I was too young. It's a good thing she didn't listen because here we are, many years later, happy as two little razor clams.

I'm older now and I have single friends in their thirties who tell me they'd *never* date someone under thirty. Never? I ask. I proceed to tell them a sweet little Texas love story, that I was twenty-five and she was thirty-five when we met. They listen, but I don't think they really get it. Love is subjective and setting parameters around who you will or will not date will only make finding someone that much harder. (Legal limits excluded.)

Be open to life! Don't listen to your jaded friends. And certainly don't turn away a great catch because she was born twelve months too late!

CHAPTER SIX

Baggage

It comes in all different sizes, colors, and styles—your baggage. If it was stuff you picked up in your youth, it's typically patent leather, like the little shoes mom made you wear. If you got them in high school, they probably have band stickers on them and a cigarette burn or two. If they came in later life, they really vary in style. If you were scorned by an ex-lover, there might be blood on your baggage, or if it was jealousy that broke up your last four relationships, baggage with teardrop stains also comes in all shades of green. Whatever you or your new girl's baggage looks like, it can be a heavy burden to carry around. The following chapter will help you understand our luggage.

Broken Beer Bottles

Jealousy

Lipstick: I threw a beer bottle at an ex-girlfriend once. (You remember Double D?) It was a moment, a sensation I'll never forget as the Amstel Light left my fingers. Double D had tried to run me over with her new BMW earlier in the night, but I was still mortified by the monster our closeted love affair pulled out of me. Double D wasn't even in the room, but I threw the bottle at the door she'd just slammed shut. I'll also never forget her face when she opened it back up to confirm what she thought she'd heard. Her eyes told me that she hated me.

DIPSTICK: Holy shit, Lip, you never told me that story. I've never seen your temper before. You're usually so Zen.

Lipstick: Me neither. And fortunately, I haven't seen it since that night, when I finally left her for good.

There were lots of emotions and reasons and circumstance that drove us to this level of angst—to a violent head that scared the shit out of both of us—but at its source was the hellhole of the closet. Just because our jealous rage was rooted in closet pressure doesn't diminish its effects, nor does it diminish how often it shows up in our other relationships. Closet or no closet, jealousy is like cancer, an insidious irritant that can kill you.

For those of you wondering what happened to me and Double D, I'll have you know we've mended the fence and are (in typical lesbo fashion) the closest of friends now. Even though I swore I wouldn't, I did throw something at her again, and it was just last weekend. It was my rubber flip-flop. I launched it across her gay West Hollywood pool as she was taking an afternoon siesta on an inflatable raft. Texas and I were visiting for a long weekend. The bonk on the head this time wasn't a jealous rage, but instead a wake-up call. It was time to hit happy hour at the Abbey!

DIPSTICK: How is DD, Lip? Did you tell her I said hi?

I agree that jealousy is a green-eyed demon that's broken up more relationships than anything else, except cheating.

Lipstick: But oftentimes they're connected.

DIPSTICK: True. A little jealousy is normal. Your girl is hot and you want to keep her. Here are some signs your jealousy has gotten out of control:

1. You've called her a cunt.
2. You call her mother to make sure she's really heading home, not to meet up with the cute girl from the coffee shop.
3. You call her cell phone more than ten times an hour.
4. You secretly check her e-mail and IM friends list.
5. You have your friend drive by her job to make sure she's really at work.

If this sounds like you, get therapy immediately. If you're superjealous, it makes your partner feel like you don't trust her because . . . you don't. If you can't trust your partner, your relationship is never going to work. Too much jealousy will only push her away, the exact opposite of what you want. Right, Lipstick?

Lipstick: Right on, Dip. There's nothing less sexy than jealously. It shows undeniable insecurity, and desperation is ugly. Nothing good can come from being jealous. Not to mention that little green bastard can drive both of you crazy. Jealousy is suffocating. There are many ways romantic jealousy manifests in our lives. Are any of these people shades of you?

Irrational Irma. Don't you hate it when you're being unreasonable, even to yourself? You know better, like you shouldn't be kneeling in the laurel bushes (not only because you're spying on your lover, but also because mud stains are hard to get out), but you just can't help yourself. You know that installing surveillance equipment in her office is completely extreme, but you find yourself there on the weekend reading installation instructions as you fasten a bug to the inside of her pencil drawer.

Linda the Lunatic. Linda the Lunatic is a step above (or below) Irma. Most women start as Irrational Irmas, and then move to complete madness. Have you ever lost your mind because of jealousy? It's a horrible, terrifying feeling—especially if it festers in someone who's insecure—right on the edge of sanity, where you're left wondering, in your fleeting moment of clarity, do I need a straight jacket?

DIPSTICK: Lip, you forgot Whimpering Wilma, the one who doesn't hide behind dumpsters or get that cat scratch fever look in her eyes, but the one whose eyes are bloodshot from crying the whole time you're apart because she's sure you're cheating.

Lipstick: Right, of course, Wilma.

Get to the root

There are typically two causes of romantic jealousy. The first may be created by your partner. She's either a cheater, has a pattern of cheating, or she's a flirt and/or liar. The second is created by you. Your insecurity won't allow you to believe that she would ever be faithful, that you were worth her being faithful, that surely she's constantly looking for something better. Or maybe you're damaged goods. You've been cheated on or you grew up in a broken home, where one of your parents strayed. All of this affects how you're currently relating to your girlfriend.

Oftentimes, the two are not solely responsible for your ravenous jealousy, but they rub together, one festering the other until, God forbid, your tragic story ends up on *Dateline*.

What can you do?

You can put down the binoculars and get your shit together. Jealousy is your reaction when your relationship is threatened, whether real or imagined. The trick is determining whether your relationship is truly threatened or if you've got your apprehensive panties in a twist for nothing. The best thing to do is talk to your girlfriend about what you're going through. Lay it all on the line with the reasons why you feel vulnerable. Well, except I wouldn't tell her about that private detective you hired; that might freak her out.

During this discussion, pay careful attention. How she reacts and how you feel might be clear indicators of where the jealousy is coming from. If she freaks out and is superdefensive maybe she's guilty of something. If she passively denies it, but her eye is twitching, you might want to keep probing. What I think will happen—unless you're already too far gone— is that you'll clearly see if what you're feeling is imagined. Sometimes it takes actually speaking the words of your reality—explaining your insatiable suspicion—for you to realize that you're being unreasonable. If you come to no conclusion, or at least aren't headed toward one, then waste no time getting in touch with a couples counselor to help you ferret out the problem.

A pinch of jealousy is good

Beyond the extreme ways jealousy manifests, a small amount of jealousy is normal and somewhat healthy. I don't think that red alert that goes off at a bar when someone is moving in on your girl is jealousy—it's territorialism and there's certainly nothing wrong with being territorial. In fact, I encourage it not only with your girlfriend, but also with friends. We must be fiercely loyal and protective when it comes to them, too. Both can be hard to find, so protect them with a loaded handgun. (I'm speaking metaphorically, of course.) That's certainly not to say your girlfriend can't talk to others or you should go ape shit when another woman approaches her. In fact, take it as a compliment. If the dumb dyke doesn't get the hint or gets pushy, then it may be time to take action, but never anything physical. There may be one thing less sexy than jealousy, come to think of it. It's a woman who gets in fistfights.

DIPSTICK: I don't know. I saw two chicks fighting once and thought it was kind of sexy, especially since their brawl was about me.

Lipstick: You remind me of Narcissus—he liked it when women fought over him, too.

DIPSTICK: Whatever. Aside from all this, jealousy is just poison anyway and never does any good. People do cheat, and I can't think of one case where jealousy has stopped someone from cheating.

Lipstick: In fact, the jealousy probably pushed them even closer to Pandora's box!

My brother (who I'll call Swami) gave me some great advice once. Years ago, I called him, afraid my girlfriend at the time was unhappy and getting ready to cheat on me (turns out she was just going through an early midlife crisis!). In response, I'd been putting extra pressure on her, getting jealous at inopportune times, and just generally being pathetic about her leaving me. Swami let me vent all my fears and pent-up angst like a wise sibling should and then told me something that truly changed my life. He said at some point, you have to let go of your fears and just allow her to cheat. "Huh?" I said.

He explained: "If she's gonna do it, there's nothing you can do to stop her. If it's going to happen, it's going to happen. Speculating and worrying about it beforehand is pointless; it's only going to make you crazy. If she does stray, then you can deal with it then."

Suddenly, a light went on inside and I said, "Aha!" He was right! So, I stepped back and stopped putting so much undue pressure on our relationship, and slathering on my excessive jealousy by being ridiculously possessive, and something magical happened. Things got better and I stopped worrying about it. Someone needed to give me permission to release my grip.

So, here I am, jealous bones, giving you permission to let go of the fear and focus on other areas of your life. Like Dipstick and Swami said, your jealous rages aren't going to stop her from getting into the fire; quite the contrary—they're going to shove her all the way in.

She Won't Stop Crying

Depression

Kit came home from work one day to find her partner Stella crying on the couch. Kit was alarmed. "What's wrong, honey?" she wanted to know. Stella could barely sniffle out, "I don't know." Kit started to panic and thought Stella was planning on leaving her. She had noticed that Stella had been distant lately, was having trouble sleeping, and didn't want to go out with their friends. Whenever she asked what was bothering her, Stella would just shrug her shoulders and say she didn't know. Kit also noticed Stella was overly upset about things she considered inconsequential, like it raining on the day they had planned to go hiking. After a comment a coworker made, Stella sulked around for days, saying she was no good and that she sucked at her job, even though Kit knew Stella regularly got great performance reviews. Kit was at her wit's end. She didn't know what to do to help Stella.

DIPSTICK: Depression is very real and difficult for all those involved. Someone who is depressed may not even know it. According to WebMD .com these are some things to look out for:

- Sadness
- Loss of enjoyment from things once pleasurable
- Loss of energy
- Feelings of hopelessness or worthlessness
- Difficulty concentrating
- Difficulty making decisions
- Insomnia or excessive sleep
- Stomachache and digestive problems
- Sexual problems (for example, decreased sex drive)
- Aches and pains (such as recurrent headaches)

- A change in appetite causing weight loss or gain
- Thoughts of death or suicide

Tiger occasionally gets the blues, so I know firsthand how difficult it can be. As a partner of someone who is depressed, here are some things you should know:

Depression is an illness. Depression is a physical, chemical, and emotional imbalance. Your partner needs to be treated, whether that involves therapy, medication, or both. Support her getting help.

It's important for you to understand she can't just "snap out of it" or "stop feeling sorry for herself." Although things like exercise and getting off the couch might make her feel better in the short term, it is not a cure for depression.

Don't judge her, call her lazy, uninspired, or unmotivated. These things will not help; they will only make her feel worse.

There are several kinds of depression. Some people get depressed in the winter months, some may be situational, like when a parent dies, and some depression is chronic. If your partner has chronic depression, it's good for you to know what you're in for.

Chronic depression. With chronic depression, your girlfriend will have good days and bad days. Educate yourself, talk to her therapist about things you can do to help. While you're being proactive, it's important to understand that you can't cure her. She has to help herself and some days, trust me, it'll seem like she won't be able to do that.

Find support for yourself. You're not being a traitor if you talk to a friend about how her depression is hard on you. For heaven's sake, don't let her bring you down, too.

Lipstick: While I know what you say is true, Dipstick, your advice makes me depressed. Back in college, I used to live with someone who struggled with depression and let me tell you, it's scary, unpredictable shit. Sometimes she wouldn't leave her room for days, and when she did, she was still in the dark—if you know what I mean. It was like she turned into a different person.

From living with her, I've learned about the signs, too. Here are some Dipstick left out:

- She hasn't washed her hair in over a week and there's so much grease you could butter your cookie sheet with one swipe.
- Instead of good morning, she tells you to fuck off.
- She's starting to stink, so much, in fact, that your cats are trying to cover her up.

DIPSTICK: If your partner has any of these signs, you should both seek counseling.

The Shane Effect

Cheating

DIPSTICK: So, you caught your lover cheating. The bitch! Let me at her!

After I'm through with her, what are you going to do? Here are your few options:

Deal with it. Either you put up with it or you don't. Either you give her another chance or you don't. It all depends on how much you feel like you can trust her. Did she tell you she was cheating, or did you catch her in the act? If she came clean, chances are, she's remorseful and wants to change. If you discovered it, the sly dog will only try to hide her tracks better next time, so beware.

Lipstick: You should *never* "put up with it" as Dipstick suggests. If she cheats on you once, then shame on her. If you let her cheat on you again, then shame on you! A third time? You're a fool who deserves it.

DIPSTICK:

Wait and see. Once your girlfriend cheats on you, it can be hard to know whether you'll ever trust her again. You can take her back and wait and see, however, some relationships recover from cheating, others do not.

Sometimes the cheating happens because there's a core issue that one partner (or both) needs to deal with. Whether it's the lack of sex in the relationship, drug or alcohol abuse, or fear of commitment, the problem must be dealt with before you can move forward.

Open the relationship up. If she's proven that she can't be with just one woman, then perhaps it's time you both took other lovers. Open relationships work for some people—see section Jean, Joan, and Me—but definitely not others.

Once when I was heartbroken over a girl who was treating me wrong, my father shared his wise words with me: "It's either going to be more painful to stay with her or more painful to leave. The decision is yours." Granted, it took a few more months of pain before I did finally leave the cheating slut, but Dad was right! Leaving her was the best thing that ever happened to me, even though it hurt like hell.

When your wandering girl comes back to you and you go cry your heart out to your friends, they are going to tell you one thing: Leave her because you deserve better than that.

You know what, they're right.

Lipstick: That's a lame cliché, Dip—everyone always says that. "You deserve better." While that may be true (or maybe you're a good-for-nothing piece of shit who's cheated a hundred times yourself), I'd like everyone to stop saying it. Can you do that for me, lesbians? It's overused and has lost its luster.

Instead of telling the next heartbroken friend who comes to you with her crying, cheated-on heart that she's deserves better, why not instead be honest with her about her mealy-mouthed unfaithful lover. Tell her the truth: that you hated her monobrow and the shoes that she wore (you *never* wear flats when you're 5'1"), or that you loathed her politics and every time she went off on a tangent about how Condoleezza Rice should be president, you wanted to bitch-slap her across the table.

Anyway, where was I? Oh yeah. Once Dipstick's done with your cheating girlfriend, send her to me. After I tear her a new asshole, here are a few other options for you to mull over:

Dump her ass. Sometimes a girl just needs to be dumped. She knows it, your friends know it, and deep down, you know it, too. Why draw out something that isn't working? Is the old adage true? Once a cheater, always a cheater? You decide.

Have your own affair. Payback's a bitch, right? Well, if your honey has stepped out on you, then sometimes it's best to go ahead and step out, too. I'd advise you to talk to her before you head out on your field trip; otherwise, you're no better than she. An eye for an eye. A poon for a poon. Bring on the payback pussy!

Resent her for years. This is the worst option of them all and, unfortunately, one option which many who have kids or have been together for over a decade choose.

"I can't imagine life without her!"

"It's for the kids!"

So you stay, and for the next decade, you hate her guts. Don't be this person. Your kids will respect you far more in the end if you leave, and besides, no matter how old you are, there's time to find a new lesbian to love, someone who treats you right because *you deserve better!*

DIPSTICK: Lip, you didn't!

Lipstick: I did, but that was just for shits and giggles, to make sure you were on your toes.

The final option is much softer and gentler:

Forgive. Why not try to forgive her? I know, a crazy concept, but you've probably done some things you don't want her to know about, right? And surely you hope she'd forgive you if you tripped and your hands slipped down someone's panties. We aren't infallible, after all. I encourage you to forgive (if you can), but only once; like I said, never forgive a second affair. Get out your burliest boots and kick her ass to the curb.

I Suck

Dealing with low self-esteem

"There is overwhelming evidence that the higher the level of self-esteem, the more likely one will be to treat others with respect, kindness, and generosity."

—NATHANIEL BRANDON

Lipstick: I can't stress enough how important healthy self-esteem is in a relationship. It sustains you when you feel alone, it attracts your partner to you, it makes you more successful, helps you fulfill your dreams, aids in building the life you want together, and nurtures the sacred bond you share.

By definition, *self-esteem* is a realistic respect for or favorable impression of oneself. Translated: you think you fucking rock.

There are a lot of reasons people are insecure, but gay people are faced with even bigger challenges when it comes to maintaining a healthy level of self-esteem. Perhaps you were constantly slapped with criticism and pressure in your youth; maybe you had horrible teenage years, ones heavy with confusion, alienation, and rejection; perhaps your insecurities continue to build as you face your midlife alone or with a trail of relationship failures; perhaps the size of your boobs is strangely out of proportion to the rest of your body.

Self-esteem is tied to the closet door handle

Are you out of the closet? I mean *fully* out of the closet? Translated: Are there people in your life who don't know you're gay or bisexual? (Your dry cleaner and the cable guy excluded.) If so, then you've got work to do because your self-esteem isn't at its full potential. Sure, you may feel confident most days, but in those moments when you struggle to keep your head high, you think being gay is something to hide, that being gay—an orientation you had *no* control over—is something to be ashamed of.

If this is you, start with your sexuality first when trying to enhance self-worth. So much is tied to our sexual orientation, especially in this media-frenzied age, where we read in the blogs or hear on talk radio that sectors of society still think we're morally reprehensible. That can be a hard pill to swallow for even the most secure homos. Focus on self-love, on getting comfortable with yourself and with your identity. It's not something that happens overnight, but with hard work and serious soul searching, it can be done.

Second, get a journal and start writing. Writing is supertherapeutic and will open up cavities in your soul that have never been tapped. It's remarkable. One important caveat: You MUST lock up this journal in order to be totally honest on its pages (a file cabinet works well). Knowing someone might find it will be a subconscious censor. Lock 'em up and you'll be amazed at the permission it grants you to explore your insecurities and the dark corners of your inner world.

Last, go buy Thom Rutledge's book *The Self-Forgiveness Handbook*.

What a gem this is. It will help you work through all sorts of baggage and set you off on a journey that will take you from self-criticism to self-compassion, which is essential to building your self-worth.

Myths about low self-esteem

- It's your parents' fault.
- Your poor fashion sense is to blame.
- It's because you're gay.
- It's all about that hairstyle you had in the eighties.
- Nothing can be done to improve it.

According to researchers at the University of Texas, there are three faces of low self-esteem. Of course, I added my own Lipstickness to them, but much of their hard work has been paraphrased here:

The Impostor: This lesbo acts happy and successful, but is really terrified of failure. She lives with the constant fear that other dykes will find out she's hurting and lost. This dyke needs incessant success—like kissing a different girl each weekend at the dyke bar—to maintain the mask of positive self-esteem, which may lead to problems with perfectionism, procrastination, competition, and burnout.

The Rebel: You rebels act like the opinions or goodwill of others—especially people who are important or powerful like Lipstick—don't matter. You'd *never* come to us for advice and you're constantly angry about not feeling good enough, continuously needing to prove that others' judgments and criticisms don't hurt. This kind of nasty, low-confidence behavior often manifests in the way you blame others excessively, break rules or laws, or fight authority.

The Loser: Oh, we've heard from more of you girls than anyone else. With the veil of the Internet between us, you write to us because you feel you can't cope. You often use self-pity or indifference as a shield against fear of taking responsibility for changing your destructive, inhibiting patterns. Because you'll hardly make a move without others' guidance, you lack assertiveness skills and are an underachiever.

DIPSTICK: If you don't see yourself in any of these faces, do any of these sound familiar?

- You're jealous of your friends' achievements.
- You drink or eat too much when you're feeling low.
- You feel like you constantly need reassurance from your partner that she loves you.
- You feel like she deserves better than you.
- You have a hard time accomplishing the things you set out to do.
- You judge yourself harshly.

If this is the case, you're probably suffering from low self-esteem. Like Lipstick said, dykes with low self-esteem depend on others too much for their self-worth. They're always judging themselves against people's achievements instead of what they've accomplished themselves. Being with someone who has low self-esteem can be draining.

You need to learn how to be your own person, create your own self-worth and direction. Here are some tips for improving your self-esteem:

Decide you want to change. Believe that you can. Change happens the moment you decide to change. It may not happen overnight, but little by little you can improve your self-esteem.

Take note. Write down every time someone gives you a compliment or you do something that you're proud of. Review this when you are feeling low.

Make a list. List all the things about your character that make you a good person. You're a loyal friend. You go out of your way to help people. You're honest and value your integrity. Also, make a list of all the accomplishments you're proud of. Did you graduate with high grades? Nurse your mother through cancer? Volunteer at the local animal shelter? You may be surprised at the amazing things you've done.

Listen to your self-talk. Pay attention to what your inner voice is saying. When you walk into a room full of lesbians, do you think, "I'm fatter than everyone here"? Or "I'm sure no one is going to talk to me"? When these little voices creep in, gently ask them to leave and replace them with a more positive message. "I look great in this outfit." Or "I'm going to talk to someone new today."

Pamper yourself. You deserve it. Make yourself a nice dinner, not just when you're having guests. Make time in your day for activities you enjoy, even if your partner doesn't want to participate. Go to a movie, a play, or a museum. Feel good about yourself for taking the risk and doing it.

Learn from your mistakes. People with low self-esteem get down on themselves whenever they do something wrong. People with high self-esteem look at their mistakes and learn from them. If you've messed up in some way, don't take it to heart. Vow to do better next time and move on.

Reward your accomplishments. Set a goal for yourself and when you achieve it, treat yourself to something you want.

Ask your friends. They're usually eager to tell you something nice, so let them share what they value about you and what makes you a great friend. Try seeing yourself through someone else's eyes.

Talk to a therapist or counselor. A professional can help you get to the root of your low self-esteem issues.

No matter what your struggles are regarding self-esteem, remember that it must be constantly cared for. Once you get healthy self-esteem, don't turn your back and think your work is done—it's easy for dark spots to grow, so always be watchful. Take good care and remember there's no one else like you on the planet and you have much to contribute.

Why Do Those Faggy Queens Need to Flaunt It?

Internalized homophobia

Lipstick: In 2006, Rosie O'Donnell made the following comment on *The View*: "Radical Christianity is just as threatening as radical Islam in a country like America."

In response, some dyke—Boobface13— who I met in a chat room discussing politics told me that she was a pro-life/Republican/Catholic lesbian and that Rosie didn't speak for her or her partner. She said Rosie should stick to TV and comedy.

Before I was able to respond, I lost my signal at the coffee shop (that lucky bitch!), but here's the gist of what I was going to say in response: While I respect Boobface13's opinion and love (god, I mean *love*) that we have the freedom of speech (surely I've said something in this book which pissed you off, or am getting ready to!), the first thing I'd like to say to Boobface13—or is that you, Mary Cheney?—is whaaa?

Q: How can a lesbian in this day and age, in this political climate, be a pro-life lesbian?

A: Internalized homophobia.

Sure, it's OK to be Catholic; in fact, plenty of my friends (along with all their guilty baggage) are surviving Catholics. Come to think of it, I know a handful of other Catholics who are gay, but just haven't admitted it. So, kudos to you for coming to terms with labia-lovin' ways. But how can you honestly subscribe to the Republican agenda? Yeah, I know there was once a day when the Log Cabin Republicans had a following—certainly they're hurting for members these days—but how can you (in good faith) still buy into the Republican propaganda when they've turned a corner and have been taking aim at us? No longer is their platform simply about putting more money in your Gucci purse, it's about stripping us of rights.

Sure, maybe you were born with a silver spoon up your ass and their economic platform makes sense to you, but how can that be a bigger issue than the fact the Republican party has (and continues to try) to demoralize us? I mean, switch the fucking channel from Fox to BBC and get a clue.

DIPSTICK: Forget the BBC—check out *Democracy Now!* and my hero, Amy Goodman. She speaks truth! Lip, the Democrats aren't out there waving the rainbow flag either.

Lipstick: Well, at least they're not burning it in effigy.

Boobface13, Rosie wasn't even talking about your conservative pussy. She was talking about the right-winger types who sling hate our way and blow up innocent people at abortion clinics, not some anal-retentive neophyte and her philistine girlfriend. Don't even get me started about you being pro-life.

DIPSTICK: Wow, Lipstick, there's that temper again.

Lipstick: I call it passion, Dip.

DIPSTICK: Boobface13 sure needs to have her head looked at, but in a way, I kind of feel bad for her. She can't help what she was taught as a child. I bet she still lives in the same conservative town she was raised in and attends mass each week with her folks.

Clearly what Boobface13 is dealing with is internalized homophobia, but do you also suffer from this obvious affliction? Or does your H-phobia creep into your life in more subtle ways? Take Dipstick's quiz to see:

Internalized homophobia or not?

Scenario 1: It's a beautiful fall evening and you're walking down the street with your lover, holding hands. A group of college-age guys turns the corner in front of you and she suddenly drops your hand and moves away. Internalized homophobia or not?

Scenario 2: Her parents are coming to visit. She goes through the house and collects every one of your *On Our Backs* magazines and lesbian sex manuals and puts them in a box, labels it "school papers," and sticks it on the top shelf of the garage. Internalized homophobia or not?

Scenario 3: You're at the park with your puppy and your girlfriend. A ten-year-old girl and her parents come up and she asks if she can pet your furry friend. Then the girl asks you whose dog it is. You tell her it's both of yours. "Oh, you must be sisters, then," she states. You don't say anything. Internalized homophobia or not?

Scenario 4: Your partner refuses to go to Gay Pride because she hates all those "big butches on motorcycles and nelly queens with three-inch heels and bouffant wigs." Internalized homophobia or not?

Homophobia is the fear, hatred, or negative attitudes toward gays, lesbians, and bisexuals. Internalized homophobia is when we take all the messages that we are bombarded with from our families, culture, and churches and turn them on ourselves. We may think we're perverted for wanting to see our lover pole-dance in a G-string. We may think we're going to hell for falling in love with another woman. We may think our parents are going to disapprove or we'll lose our friends.

It's easy to blame the outside world for homophobia, but what about when those same feelings exist inside us? Internalized homophobia is natural to some degree. Scenarios 1, 2, and 3 are all things that have happened to me. Why did I drop my lover's hand when a group of frat boys came rowdily toward us? Fear of being gay-bashed.

Why did I hide all the sex books when my family came to visit? No one wants her parents to see what sex books she's reading, no matter what her sexual orientation. I didn't hide the *Curve* magazines (I put them on top) or my lesbian pulp novel collection. I didn't take down the Dyke March poster or the photos of my wife and me on our wedding day. I just didn't want Dad asking me about labia piercing or my mom wondering what sex toys we enjoy most.

As for the little girl, she was just so proud of herself for figuring it out, that I didn't have the heart to correct her. Afterward Tiger and I discussed the pros and cons of telling versus not telling her. Since this was right after we were married and gay marriage was all over the news, we could have easily said, "We're not sisters, we're married." We didn't that time, but in the future we might.

Scenario 4 is clearly internalized homophobia. If you think flamboyant sissies or labrys-toting bull dykes reflect negatively on you, then you've got some work to do. All gays and lesbians are not straight-laced bankers and lawyers. The diversity and flamboyancy of our community is what makes it so wonderful. Sure, there are members of the LGBT clan I would rather not associate with, but that does not mean they don't have a place in our world. It would just be egotistical to think their behavior reflected on me and how I live my life.

Lipstick, have you calmed down yet?

Lipstick: Yes, I'm totally Zen again, thanks for the break. Regarding the stinkeye many queers flash the flamboyant sissies and bull dykes, I disagree with you, Dip. I think they do reflect who we are as a community, and that can be the tricky thing when it comes to dealing with those honest feelings that pop up. We say we want the world to accept all of us and not pass their judgment on the BDSM guy on the cover of the local paper after Pride, but that's just what they do. Mainstream folks judge us by what they see on the news, which, I might add, is always the most shocking clip they can capture.

So, I challenge all of you who find flamboyancy and colorful individuality within our community repulsive to get your butt off the lounge chair—the one in your duct-taped circle on the sidelines of the Pride Parade—and start a contingency of your own: Law Lovin' Lesbos, Daredevil Dykes,

Rug Munchin' Number Crunchers. Think of some catchy title for your group and get marching! Represent!

DIPSTICK: Seems like even Lipstick has a bit of internalized homophobia. I'm working on her though . . .

When You're Just Her "Friend"

The closet

Tammy worked as a longshoreman for ten years and loved her job. She enjoyed being out in the open air, the physical work, and being a part of the union. Tammy was the only woman working the docks at her job, but she didn't mind. She got along great with the guys, sometimes meeting them after work for a beer. Every year the company hosted a Labor Day picnic, and Tammy was usually involved in organizing it and played shortstop on the softball team. After three years together, Tammy finally invited Jasmine to the company picnic. Jasmine was shocked to hear Tammy introduce her around to her coworkers as her "roommate." Jasmine had no idea Tammy was not out at work and she couldn't understand it.

DIPSTICK: As far as Dipstick is concerned, there are only two reasons to be in the closet: if you're in the military or if you risk losing custody of your children. And even the military is a weak excuse. Some people think they need to be in the closet for work, but that's a cop-out. While it is true that, in many states, you can be fired from your job just for being a lesbian, is having the job worth the self-sacrifice of putting on a heterosexual mask, not to mention stockings and heels, day after day, pretending to love Dick, when all you do is daydream about Jane? Even if you're a Hollywood millionaire, no amount of money can compensate for the anemic, air-deprived, stifling closet.

I say all of us gays and lesbians burst into our bosses' offices today and announce that we're queer. What will happen if we're all fired and end up on unemployment? The tax burden itself will force Congress into passing an employment nondiscrimination law. Now that's progress!

Lipstick: While I'm all about being out and proud and agree there are few good reasons to be in the closet, we mustn't pressure someone out until they're ready. It takes time to admit to yourself that you're gay and that you're attracted to women. But once you do, here are some helpful tips from my own experience of coming out to the world. For both the dyke in the closet, as well as her partner, I've cooked up a scrumptious meal just for your special soul called Lipstick Soup. It may not sound very appetizing, but trust me, it's good for you. Here's your helping.

Lipstick Soup for the Closeted Soul

Following my first lesbian experience, it took me three years to finally come out of the closet. Growing up, I had no idea I was gay. Well, not consciously. I knew I was different. Now, in queersight, I can see my sexuality chasing me around the playground and woven into every relationship I've ever had. Even after I fell in love with Double D, my sacred first, and had been in a closeted relationship for almost two tumultuous years, I wasn't ready to admit to myself that I was gay. Isn't that fucked up?

It took me a long time to finally get to the core, to peel the final layer of shame back so I could see that I was a frickin' lesbian. Before that insanely epic night—when my pen first wrote the words "I'm gay" in my journal—I'd thought the love affair Double D and I were having was just a really intimate friendship gone awry. Have you had one of those?

If this sounds familiar, and you're still in the closet to yourself or loved ones (even though you may be in a relationship), be patient with yourself, but know that it's tough to get to a place where it's a totally comfortable experience. One place you do need to get to is that spot where you're ready to lose everything, no matter what, to stand in the truth of who you are.

And you must remember, sweet sister, that you are not alone. Ever. We've all braved the scalding licks of coming out hellfire before you. The path is beaten and you will always have family in the dyke community, especially if you temporarily or permanently lose yours in the process.

Be sure. You need to be completely confident in your sexuality before you come out to the world. The last thing you want is for someone to try to confuse you. I had many people ask if I was sure, that it might be a phase. If I'd still been in that shaky place where I wasn't actually sure—I mean really sure—then it could've been jarring. Get cozy in that new skin first and build a support system around you that goes further than your girlfriend.

Be prepared with a plan. I went into my coming out with a very detailed plan, which included plenty of time and space to tell each friend and family member on the list.

DIPSTICK: That's so you, Lipstick. You are such a goal-setting, charted course kind of girl.

Lipstick: I know, I can't help myself.

"Always plan ahead. It wasn't raining when Noah built the arc." (Richard Cushing)

I'd like to add to that quote:

"Always plan ahead. It wasn't raining when Noah built the arc, just like Lipstick wasn't in the fetal position and weeping like a child when she imagined coming out to her parents."

Because that's what happened when I finally got to those two little words—"I'm gay." It wasn't pretty. Thank God I wrote a letter and had it in my back pocket, just in case. I wasn't sure I'd be able to keep it together, and damn was I ever right. When the moment came to tell each of them— even though they're happily married, I told them separately—I couldn't speak.

Fortunately, I was able to pull out my note and read it. Dad took the letter before I finished my lamenting monologue—before I got to the really important part—and said, "I know."

DIPSTICK: Your dad is so cool!

Lipstick: I know! So is my mom—she is a rock.

Be ready for anything. My dad's reaction surprised me. In fact, a lot of people's reactions surprised me. My dad began crying with me, but not because he was sad for selfish reasons—his daughter was gay, how embarrassing, or where did he go wrong—he was crying because he was sad that I'd had to carry my burden alone. "I wish I could've been there for you all those years when you were struggling," he said. My mom also surprised me. She was as strong as an ox when I told her, more concerned about the sobbing coma I was slipping in and out of than her own well-being. She told me that she loved me and it didn't matter. Consoling me in the face of my own demons, she was my strength. It was only weeks later that some issues bubbled up for her, things that she had to deal with on her own in the first year I was out of the closet. And now, they both continue to amaze me with their undying support. Texas and I got married several years ago, and they were on the first plane to be there for the ceremony, not to mention they then threw us a reception with a hundred of their nearest and dearest friends, 99 percent of whom are steadfast Republicans!

DIPSTICK: Maybe some of them switched teams after your ceremony—to Democrat, that is.

Lipstick: Oh there was the other kind of team switching, too. By the end of the night, one of my straight friends was macking down with one of my dyke friends. Ask my dad; I saw him see the whole thing as he was putting another log on the fire. I'm not sure whose eyes were bigger, mine or his!

Lipstick Soup for the Partner's Soul

I've been in your shoes, too, patient one. While it may be hard for us to understand how or why our lover is in the closet with certain people, it's important to be loving and supportive. That's not to say you shouldn't encourage her and help her get to a comfort zone. That's also not to say that you can't feel frustrated at times, angry even, especially when the closet door infringes on your life.

Back before Texas, I dated a woman who took me home for Christmas one year. She came from a conservative Christian family who lived in a small Midwestern town and their invitation was monumental. Here was the snag: Even though I was invited, I was still just her "friend" to her grandparents. This ex-girlfriend of mine swore—practically on her life—many, many years ago that she wouldn't tell her grandparents she was gay . . . and her mom is holding her to it. And this chick was typically an alpha—no one told her what to do, including me (if you can believe that!)—but this situation was a sticking point for her and a definite trigger in our relationship. She insisted she didn't have a choice. I insisted she did. Needless to say, this caused more than one spat, always involving tears, but

I came to realize that it wasn't my place to interfere with her family dealings. I could tell her how I felt and how it was affecting me and then try to let go of my anger. I mean what else could I do besides go for long runs and drink lots of wine?

Be supportive. Be nothing but supportive of your girl if she's coming out of the closet. If possible—and some days it's challenging—don't put pressure on her, or make her feel guilty because you think she should be out already. Be loving and patient and give her what she needs. Ask if it's not clear and never ever, ever, ever take it upon yourself to out her. In the end, even though progress is important—she shouldn't stay in the closet for the rest of her life— and it comes down to the choices she makes, your job first is to be supportive.

DIPSTICK: We recently heard from Jane from Jasper, Indiana.

Jasper Jane and her family's river of denial

Jane's mom calls to talk once a week. The two of them catch up on family gossip and the weather in their respective cities. Even though Jane and Irma have been together for fourteen years, her mom never asks about Irma. Occasionally Jane will mention Irma getting a promotion at work or some other piece of good news, and her mom always responds in the same way, "It's so nice that you and Irma are such good friends." Although Jane came out to her mother fifteen years ago, she insists on believing Jane and Irma are nothing more than friends.

Perhaps your partner's parents are not in as deep denial as Jane's but it sure can hurt to always be referred to as the "friend." There are two possibilities of why this is happening:

1. Your partner has no spine and refuses to tell her parents that you're her lesbian lover.
2. Your partner reminds her family every time they speak who you are and what you mean to her, but they choose not to hear it.

Lipstick: I'd like to add two more:

1. Her parents think she's a LUG (Lesbian Until Graduation) and that she'll eventually outgrow it.

2. They're terribly insecure and choose to penalize you both for their own emotional deficiencies by living in denial, convinced those around them—neighbors, friends, and family members—don't have a clue. Joke's on them: Everybody knows!

DIPSTICK: Denial as strong as with Jane and her mom is hard to overcome. Dipstick says that it's a lost battle and encourages you not to waste your energy. If they choose to ignore you, then it's time your lover stepped up to the plate. She doesn't have to go ballistic and scream that you are not just friends but that you share a bed and a number of expensive sex toys. She just needs to gently refer to you as her partner or wife every time she mentions your name.

Lipstick: God have I been there! As a femme, it's way too easy for me to be passed off as the friend.

No matter how you handle this sticky situation, no doubt there will be frustration along the way. Don't feel bad about your feelings, just talk openly with you girlfriend and, in the face of your annoyance, try to love and support her decisions. It's her life after all and you've chosen to be with her.

PART III

Intimacy and Sex

CHAPTER SEVEN

In the Bedroom

Lipstick: Let me tell you a story . . .

Back when I was a tiny closeted femme, I would've given anything for a Lesbian Sex 101 class. When Double D and I kissed for the first time we found ourselves, literally, in the dark. While our sorority sisters unwittingly pounded on my bedroom door, we fumbled in and out of each other's panties trying to balance what felt right with what we'd seen in the porno films that played in the background at high school parties. I worried I didn't have acrylic fingernails, that I had too much pubic hair, and that my high heels weren't stilettos. We didn't have a clue what lesbians did. We knew what felt good, and that was a great place to start, but our initial attempts at lovemaking can only charitably be described as the blind leading the blind.

In retrospect, I'm not surprised. There is so much mystery surrounding lesbian sex, not only for straight people, but for budding lesbians, too. Face it, dykes aren't born with a how-to manual. If you came out in the last five years you could at least run to your local bookstore or Amazon and buy one of the myriad sex manuals out there (see section Dust Off the Candles). But, that's only good for those who are out enough to keep lesbian how-to books in their dorm rooms or forward thinking enough to buy a book long before that first—possibly drunken (ours wasn't)—encounter.

The things that tickle our fancies are as diverse as the lesbian community itself. I've come a long way since Double D and I first rolled around and realize now there are endless options for lesbians, but the bottom line is *pleasure.*

Portions of this chapter were previously published in *Curve* magazine, 2005.

DIPSTICK: I agree, Lip, but it's also about connection.

If there's one thing I hate, it's when little dykelettes (and teenage boys) write in and ask what constitutes losing your virginity for lesbians. I can't say there's an easy answer, but I do contend that when you lose your virginity, you'll know it!

All Dipstick has to add to this introduction about lesbian sex is that it's our sexuality that sets us apart. Sure, it's not all of who we are, but it does define us. It's what causes religious leaders and politicians to scorn us and deny us rights. It's what gives our families reason to reject us and even causes some of us to lose our jobs. In light of that, we owe it to ourselves to have plenty of sex. So, get out there and get busy!

Dip Me in Honey and Throw Me to the Lesbians

The world of fantasies

Lipstick: If there's one thing we writers have going for us, it's our wild imaginations because this means we have three-dimensional fantasies. I don't know about you, Dipstick, but mine are so real I can sometimes actually feel Kate Winslet's nipple in my mouth when I'm masturbating. It tastes like a Sweet Tart.

DIPSTICK: You may have Kate's nipple, but I'm being handcuffed and thrown into a police cruiser by that nasty dyke cop. She's about to take me downtown and book me.

Lipstick: I bet she is. I knew your past would catch up with you eventually. Fantasies are more than OK; they're healthy and good for your sexual appetite. Your partner shouldn't feel threatened by your fantasies, and neither should you. If your girl likes to think about someone else for a brief moment during sex (she'll probably never be honest about this), then yee haw! It's not the end of the world. It doesn't mean she's going to leave you. At least she's in bed with you and not actually sleeping with the girl at the bus stop.

DIPSTICK: I remember the first time my college professor's face popped into the bedroom when I was feeling around my partner's panties. It freaked me out and I sure as hell couldn't pay attention in class the next day.

Lipstick: No kidding. I've had the strangest people show up in my fantasies. The worst is when you have a sexual dream and then have to work with that person the next day. It can be someone you've never found attractive, and then suddenly they're spread-eagle on the conference table.

The best time to really cultivate our world of fantasy is when we're masturbating. You, too, can become a creative writer, writing your fantasies on paper or in the clouds, right next to your castle in the sky, where fifty hot naked ladies wait for you. Allow yourself the freedom—free from your own internal critic, judging your every tingle—to explore your inner sex-pot. Don't freak out if your fantasies go beyond girl-on-girl action. In fact, I'd be surprised if they don't. And it doesn't necessarily mean that you want to act your fantasies out. For example, you'll never be Brian Kinney at a Miami White Party fucking every guy in sight, but it might be fun to fantasize that you are. And, you'll most likely never get the chance to sleep with Angelina Jolie, Shane from *The L Word*, or Sheryl Crow, but there's nothing wrong with having a wild imagination.

DIPSTICK: I'm still holding out for Sheryl. Yes, Lipstick, even more than when I saw my professor's face, I freaked out the first time I had a sex dream about a man. You might not guess this right off, but Dipstick is a gold star—never has a male hand even made it close to my jog bra strap. So waking up remembering what had so turned me on in the night, I panicked. I went straight to my bisexual friend Polly and told her I might be joining her team soon.

Sexually liberated that she was, Polly assured me that it was just a dream—that we're all yin/yang, male/female, and a bunch of other new age crap that really calmed me down and made me realize, just because I dreamed of sleeping with a man, didn't mean I had to do it. Whew! And I could even fantasize about Brad Pitt (with Angelina Jolie, of course!) and it didn't mean I wasn't a true gold star.

Lipstick: Here, here, Dipstick. Because I'm a tarnished star—I've slept with one dude (I'll call him Stanley, since that's what he called his deely-hoo, a tribute to the drill), someone I cared deeply about with whom I'm still friends—my dreams about men are even more realistic. I've actually had one of those big things in my hands.

DIPSTICK: Eeew!

Lipstick: Among other places. One random, hot summer night last year, I dreamt that Stanley and I were back together. I was in a white dress, surrounded by all my childhood friends and Stanley and I were getting married! Have you ever had a dream that you're in front of a firing squad? You're screaming that you're innocent, but they line up with their big rifles anyway? That's how it felt, only I was screaming "I'm a lesbian! I love Texas!" to Stanley as I was walking down the aisle. There's a difference between a fantasy and a dream, however. Fantasies you can control. Dreams, obviously, you can't. Don't be freaked out by either one. Just go with the flow.

I Miss My Strap-On

Sexual hang-ups

DIPSTICK: As lesbians, we're already regarded as perverts, outlaws, and deviants; just the fact that we prefer to snack on fleshy tacos over lap taffy makes us suspect. So, what is normal lesbian sex? There is no normal. Give me one hundred lesbians and I will show you one hundred different sexual preferences. So, what do you do when your partner doesn't like or won't participate in the very bedroom activities that send you to the moon?

Lipstick: For couples, being successful in the bedroom is all about flexibility. When I say flexibility, I don't mean if you can wrap your leg around your head (although that would be a bonus); I mean about what you're doing and how you're doing it. Each couple brings different turn-ons, turnoffs, fetishes, experiences, and inhibitions to the relationship, so the best way to find mutual satisfaction in the bedroom is to think of your bed as a steaming melting pot. Here's my favorite recipe.

Ingredients for a delicious pot of lesbian sex

4 cups of cunnilingus
1½ cup good vibrations

1 cup strap-on fun

¼ cup dildos

½ cup anal stimulation (fingers or other accoutrement)

1 tablespoon of porn

2 drops of lube

Sounds yummy, huh? You might be hungry, but beware: sexual hang-ups can spoil your simmering stew.

Inhibition and fear

Sexual hang-ups are caused by fear. Sexual abuse is a perfect example of what can induce fear, but so are many of the other issues. Are you afraid of exploring in the bedroom? Does a butt plug secretly intrigue you, but are you terrified to buy one, let alone use one? How about other fetishes you've dreamed of? All that's holding you back is that little frightened voice in your mind. Try to challenge it next time you hear it and do something daring. Surprise yourself! Those nipple clamps might be just what the doctor ordered to help you take your orgasms to the next level!

Body image

A big, so to speak, issue for lesbians is body image. Are you uncomfortable in your skin? Does the thought of being naked in broad daylight scare the hell out of you? If so, whether you're conscious of it or not, this is hampering your sex life. Body image issues aren't solely tied to weight; it may be issues about how many freckles you have or you think your hips are out of proportion to your body or that you're kitty isn't pretty. The list goes on and on. The best advice I can offer here is to get over it! The sooner you do, the better your sex life with be.

Trust

Trust is a big one, especially when it comes to bondage and role playing. The issues surrounding trust are probably not caused by your partner, but from something that happened in your past. If you find yourself not trusting your partner in the bedroom, try to take baby steps to break through that roadblock. Trust is something which can be earned in a sexual relationship. How about letting her tie you up with Velcro handcuffs or using a silk, partially see-through blindfold instead of the jet black velvet? Little by little, you'll get to that place where you can do anything behind a closed door.

Whatever your sexual hang-ups are, or whatever your partner isn't giving you, the important thing to remember is (as always) keep those lines of communication open. You can't work through something if neither of you is talking about it. Be brave and crack open that box!

She Hasn't Gone Down on Me Since 1987

When you ain't gettin' any

Lesbian Bed Death (LBD): Real or imagined? Based on the number of letters we get, it happens. It's real. And it sucks.

Lipstick: Unless there are physical or mental health issues, there's no excuse for LBD except laziness, girls. Take your reasoning and your busy schedules and your dead-end job excuses and shove 'em where the sun doesn't shine—literally. We often hear from women who complain that the sex in their relationship has waned and when they actually do feel randy, their partner doesn't. And vice versa.

The other night, after a long dinner at our favorite spot, Texas had that twinkle in her eye. I thought I saw it at the restaurant as we shared dessert, but I was certain of it when we got home; we were barely through the door when I felt her finger slide into the back of my tank top and our bodies come together.

I wasn't in the mood, but I wasn't about to throw a wet blanket over her fire. Like the players on the hit reality show *Survivor*, I, too, have learned fire is sacred and essential, and must be well taken care of.

So what happened that night?

I let her do whatever she wanted even though my full belly and I weren't feeling the "love." But let me tell you, it didn't take but thirty seconds before I too was singing *Feel Like Making Love*.

There's a very important message in my story: be careful when you shut down your horny honey. If she feels like fooling around, then, like me, you'd best just talk yourself into it. This is a precursor to LBD, if there is such a thing (I think it should be called Relationship Bed Death, because it happens just as often in gay and hetero relationships, too). Having both lovers (after they've been together for a long time) hot and bothered at the same time is like you both getting bingo in a hall of a thousand old ladies.

I know sometimes you just aren't in the mood—you're tired after a long day at the office or you have too much on your mind—and that's OK, but just don't make a habit out of saying no. Trust me, you'll be sorry when she stops asking.

DIPSTICK: Lip, glad you and your Texas rose got it on the other night—really—but I need to make one thing clear: Ladies, it is OK to say no if you're not in the mood. As women, we are so often taught that we have no right to say no. Just because you're now sleeping with a woman doesn't mean you can't refuse her.

That said, if you want to have sex, you've got to have sex. So, you'd better say yes to your sweetie every now and then. Aside from saying yes, here are a couple surefire ways to combat the dreaded LBD:

Sweetness pays off. Who wants to get all sexy with someone who degrades them, or nags about the dishes? Not me! And not her either. Treat her like the queen that she is.

Mark it on the calendar. Make sex dates. I remember being at a friend's house once and there it was, right on the calendar in their kitchen, SEX, written in big red letters. That's what I like to see. I just hope they followed through on it. Make sure you do, too. Set aside a Friday evening or Sunday afternoon. Turn off your cell phones and turn on each other. Whether you plan to spend half the day in bed or just jump on each other for a quickie doesn't matter. What matters is that you both show up and get it on.

Break the cycle. If you've fallen into a randyless rut and aren't having sex then change something. One thing. Anything. It's like that Donny Osmond album you used to have as a kid. When it got to that one part of the song *Puppy Love* and it skipped—"And they called it, And they called it, And they called it . . ."—Donny would drone on endlessly until you got up and moved the needle.

That's what you need to do now, move the needle. Buy some sex toys, rent a porno film, talk about your secret fantasy, whatever it is that's going to get you back in the bedroom and making whoopee. Keep reading and perhaps these next few sections will inspire you.

Lipstick: How could you bring Donny Osmond into this chapter? You just did the opposite of what we're trying to accomplish here—you turned off the entire lesbian community.

DIPSTICK: Yeah, that wasn't a good move, but the analogy is important: don't let the same old rhythm play over and over or you'll end up hating the song.

When It's Time to Buy Batteries in Bulk

How to deal with different sex drives

Lipstick: It's true that your sex drive changes as you age, but dating someone who's older doesn't mean that you'll be underfed or dissatisfied in bed. My Texas tornado and I are ten years apart and the age difference has never been an issue in our sex life. Either she's turbo sex charged or I not only have an old soul, but also an old libido.

DIPSTICK: Whatever that means, Lipstick. More often than not, one partner is going to have a higher sex drive than the other. Dipstick could speak to this firsthand, but Tiger won't allow her to talk about their sex life to the masses. So let me offer just a few pointers for those of you who have a higher sex drive than your true love.

Check it out. A low sex drive is one thing, but no sex drive is another. If you find yourself in this situation, go to a doctor. The problem may be physical, may be psychological, or may be medically induced. Make sure there's not a simple solution.

Talk about it. Talk to her about your needs, but not when you're turned on. Trust me on this one. If you're horny as hell and she's shot you down for the third time this week, it might not be a good time to talk. You're just going to get pissed and she's going to get defensive, pushing you even further away from the pussy.

Take care of each other. It's all about negotiation and compromise, like who gets to use the car on Wednesday and who walks the dog when it's raining. Just because you have a higher libido doesn't mean you're right, and because hers is lower doesn't mean she gets to control when you have sex. Come to an agreement that works for both of you. Every other Sunday and the fourth Thursday of the month? Mondays and Wednesdays with a quickie before softball practice on Saturday? Whatever you work out, make sure you stick to the agreement or renegotiate when needed. And don't forget to take care of her pleasure. Just because you're the horndog, doesn't mean you get to call the shots.

Take care of yourself. And by that I don't mean have an affair. Get yourself a personal massager. Start a porn collection or get some erotic books. Whatever it takes to get you off. 'Nuff said.

Lipstick: Did you really just say "'nuff said"? Just because Texas and I don't have an imbalance when it comes to libido—I count myself lucky for this—doesn't mean I haven't been there. One of my ex-girlfriends completely shut down on me right after our first anniversary. There were lots of extraneous circumstances which caused the chastity belt to come out of the drawer, but they don't matter. Lack of intimacy is the beginning of the end.

We get TONS of e-mails from women whose lovers have stopped showing up in the bedroom, either figuratively or physically. Oftentimes, their concerns include that fact that their girlfriends are superpassive about their lack of sex. There could be several reasons for this, but the big one is often depression.

Normally depression plays a big role in a diminished sex drive. Whether it's the chicken before the egg may depend on the circumstances—is she depressed because she can't ring her bell, or can she not ring the bell because she's depressed? Either way, there's a problem and you need to act fast!

Years ago, my lover was apathetic when I tried to talk to her about it. She never wanted to deal, just continued flipping through the channels, but

Lipstick's Ten Moves to Never Make in Bed

1. Never reach for the lube in the dark when Bengay is on the nightstand.
2. If you can at all avoid it, don't fart.
3. Never accidentally call out your ex-girlfriend's name.
4. Never tell her that she's a "whole lotta lovin'."
5. Never share the same dildo without washing it first or changing the condom.
6. Never be selfish, always be selfless.
7. Never let her get away without pleasing her.
8. Never be insecure about how you smell—take good care with hygiene and eat foods that are good for you and your puss.
9. Never hold back the intensity of your orgasm. Let it all out!
10. When in the bedroom, never talk about problems you're having in your relationship; it's not the time or place.

deep down, I knew she was depressed. In hindsight, I should have flushed the damn remote down the toilet and forced her to talk to me.

Learn from my mistake and take this last bit of advice: Shake your honey pie!

Not literally, of course, but don't just let her push you off when you confront her about your intimacy issues. Sure, maybe the first time you approach it, maybe even the second, but don't let her take you both down the drain of indifference. Freak out. Check for a pulse and insist that she gets off the couch and you do something proactive about it! Dipstick encouraging you to go see a professional is right on the money. It's never too soon to go see a therapist or a doctor. Find out what's wrong and fix it!

B*zzzzzzzzzzzz*

Masturbation

Lipstick: I love masturbation. Everyone—and I mean everyone—should be masturbating. Not at work, or on the city bus, but just about anywhere else. I'm such a proponent of self pleasure because when I was younger, pinned down by religious guilt, I crucified myself for what I liked to do late at night under the covers. I was taught it was wrong and so I thought each time I touched myself, I was committing a sin. The same internal abuse ensued after I slept with my first girl; I lived in denial for months that we were actually having sex—licking each other's hoo hoos and poking each other's ya yas.

DIPSTICK: So deep in denial that you couldn't even say the proper words . . .

Lipstick: Only now, after years of shoveling in my knee-high boots, have I been able to trudge through the bullshit I was force-fed during my hormonal formative years at church: it's a sin, I'm going to go to hell, and I'd best be ashamed of what my body was feeling, for what felt normal to me.

So, having left that baggage behind, I can now shout to the world that *I love to masturbate*. And so should you. Let me tell you why.

Why Lipstick loves masturbation

- A good orgasm will take away all your troubles.
- It helps me relax—it's cheaper and safer than Valium and booze.
- Because I can do it any damn time I please.
- No chance of getting herpes.
- Because I love orgasms.
- I am multiorgasmic so my fun can go on for hours and hours.
- Because Lipstick knows what Lipstick likes. God bless Texas, but nobody can fuck Lipstick like Lip can fuck Lip.
- Did I mention the orgasms?

But I'm in a relationship, you say, why would I need to masturbate?

Good question. Masturbating when in a relationship is just as important as it was when you were single. When you were a bachelorette, it was a matter of survival. Now, you're in a relationship and have a lover at your fingertips, but it's still superimportant to use those fingertips on your own yoni. Why? Because it enhances your sex life.

Additionally, there are few things as erotic as masturbating with your partner. (If you've never seen a woman masturbate until orgasm, look the f— out!). Not only is it delicious to rub one out with your girl, but it's important to stay connected to your intimate self. And your partner better not balk about it; it's perfectly normal and healthy to continue masturbating even when you're satisfied in your sexual relationship. The only time she has the right to pitch a fit is if you fall into masturbation mania and stop sleeping with her, too.

Masturbation and sex with a partner—although they have the same end result—are two very different things.

DIPSTICK: Isn't that the truth! Sometimes Dipstick just wants to let off a little steam. All the hours spent cooped up in my office writing this book, tension starts to build and I need a release. (In fact, I just had one a few minutes ago.) I certainly don't want to hold all that in until Tigerlily gets home—although sometimes, that can make for the start of a lovely evening.

So I whip out my trusty vibrating friend, conjure up that *L Word* scene with Bette and Candace in jail, and presto! Tension released, back to work.

That's not the kind of lovemaking I want to have with Tiger. I don't want to treat her as a breathing sex toy—only to get me off so I can get back to work. When we connect, I want it to be about passion, or love or fun or sharing or making up from a fight—not just physical release. Shoot, sometimes when I'm with her, I get so caught up in the give and take, I forget to have an orgasm. When it's just me, I never forget.

The Rabbit Habit

Toys, toys, toys

Lipstick: I love our little box of tricks. Texas and I keep it under her nightstand, just within her long arm's reach. In that red box, we've got purples toys and red gizmos, some that vibrate, some that swirl, and one—that we got as a gift a few years ago—that we haven't figured out how to use.

Sex toys are a delicious spice you can add to your bedroom and your love life. If you don't have any toys and have been afraid to buy one (we've heard from many women who think old-fashioned lesbian sex is the only way dykes should hump) I urge you to grab your keys and get to your local sex shop.

"What sex shop!" you scream. "I live in a tiny town in Montana."

Don't fret. If you live somewhere without a sex shop, or if it's either too nasty or too dangerous to go to, then there's yet another reason to love the Internet: There are plenty of lesbian-friendly places online where you can find your instrument of seduction. Check these sites out:

- Lesbiantoyshop.com
- Babeland.com
- Lesbiansextoys.com
- a-womans-touch.com
- twogirlsandtheirtoys.com

Don't feel too overwhelmed by the selection on some of these Web sites. There are hundreds of dildos, vibrators, and thingamabobs.

To help you navigate through the waves of pleasure, here are a few of my favorites.

Lipstick's picks

The Magic Wand. Let me tell you, this baby IS magic. When not between your or your lover's legs, it doubles as a great karaoke microphone.

The Water Dancer. Put this in your purse for a quickie in the car. There's no better way to take the edge off before a big interview or a stressful presentation at work. Get two Water Dancers and you and your lover can masturbate together before you go to bed.

The Rabbit Habit. You've got to be good and ready for this pearled, gyrating little wabbit. If you orgasm easy, the Rabbit Habit might be too much for you, but don't worry, you can adjust its speed and turn it off if there's a little too much zip in its tip. Order one of these bad girls and, like a pet rabbit, your lover will be eating out of your hand (www.rabbitvibrators.com).

DIPSTICK: Water Dancer, I'll have to Google that one. I agree with Lip. Sex toys aren't just for breakfast anymore.

Tigger and I were together five years before we brought our first toy into the bedroom. If you haven't been together five years yet, let me be the first to tell you, sex can get boring and routine. Yes, there was the brief spike that came after she got that cute little uniform from her FedEx job, but soon even that fantasy wore off.

FedEx did make one delivery, and another and another, that has added plenty of spark, and jingle, and buzz back into our sex lives.

Sex toys are just that—toys. They make sex fun again. Although sometimes I am creeped out that my wife is attracted to the animals: the vibrating duck, the rotating rabbit, and the bouncy dolphin . . . Hey, it's her fantasy. Who am I to judge?

Rewind, Pause, Slow Motion

Porn

Lipstick: Anyone who says porn doesn't turn them on is either (a) lying or (b) isn't watching the right movies. A good porno will not only get the juices flowing, but it will also spice up any romp in the hay. I highly recommend keeping a few hot titles in your bedroom stash for those nights neither of you are in the mood, but you've both scheduled time in your Outlook for sex.

Those who have been together for more than five years—long since out of the honeymoon phase—almost always have to schedule time for intimacy. And it's a good idea, too, because life can get in the way and often does. Unfortunately, when your reminder pops up on your CrackBerry, the kitty isn't always interested in coming out to play. Sometimes it just wants to take a nap or watch *Entertainment Tonight*. Help Miss Kitty along with a little nip of porn. If you're new to porn—and even if you're not—here are some things to keep in mind when you jump into the porno pool:

1. Make sure the selection you choose from the store is in English.

DIPSTICK: There's a story here, I know it!

Lipstick: Maldiga el derecho (damn right)!

2. Explore new titles. Variety is the spice of life. Don't think you have to rent solely lesbian porn just because you're a scissor kisser. You might be surprised by what floats the boat.

DIPSTICK: I don't know about you, Lipstick, but I've never found a lesbian porno that has turned me on. *If These Walls Could Talk 2*, now that's some hot shit.

Lipstick: Oh, I totally have, and that sexy miniseries with Chloe, Ellen, and Vanessa Redgrave is not porn. Lonestar and I rented a movie a few years ago that was horrible. So bad, in fact, we didn't get busy at all; just ended up laughing. Lee Press-On Nails are so not hot. In fact, I find them rather offensive. Do straight men really think lesbians only French kiss outside their mouths?

3. Mind the vagine and don't be frightened by what does turn you on. As we've said, just because you go nuts for a ménage à trois doesn't mean you're straight and it doesn't compromise your lesbian identity. In the same way, being turned on by two guys packing fudge doesn't mean you're a gay man. The vagina is its own connoisseur and even though you'd never sleep with a guy, seeing him bone some hot chick or another dude may be a turn-on; we're sexual beings after all. Don't be afraid by what you feel.

DIPSTICK: True story: The first porn I ever watched was with my college feminist collective. We were previewing the movie so we could know what we were protesting the next day when they showed the movie on campus. I don't remember the name of the film, but to this day, I can see that lady whose car broke down on the highway, forcing all the men who stopped to help her to their knees. You can bet I didn't tell the feminist collective I thought it was hot.

Lipstick: I think I've seen that one.

4. Keep toys handy. Trust me on this one. It won't take long for the lights to come on and you want to be good and ready when they do.

5. Close your bedroom door and your windows so you can have the volume up. The sounds add a richness to the gravy.

DIPSTICK: Better yet, dial into some Web porn sites. Prop that laptop up somewhere comfortable and put your headphones on. Just don't forget to empty the cache when you're through.

Lipstick: If you're looking for a little girl-on-girl action, we've got a few titles to recommend per our favorite sex shop It's My Pleasure. Here are the top three best-selling lesbian pornos: *Crash Pad*, *Sugar High Glitter City*, and *Hard Love/How to Fuck in High Heels*. (Side note: We haven't seen these.)

DIPSTICK: Don't like any of those? Make your own. Everyone has a video camera and iMovie these days. When you're done, send them to *Curve* magazine, Lipstick & Dipstick, 1550 Bryant Street, #510, San Francisco, CA 94103.

And video porn isn't the only way to go. Nothing is hotter than reading erotica out loud to each other. Check out the *Herotica* titles or *Best Lesbian Erotica* series.

Better yet, write your lover a dirty story. Even if you're not Susie Bright, reading a sexy fantasy of your own composition is sure to turn her on. Make her the star of your titillating tome and she's sure to beg you to read it to her again and again.

Get Out of My Dam Bed

Dealing with protection

If you're clueless when it comes to lesbian sex protection, you're not alone. How can I be safe? What kind of protection is out there?

Lipstick: We've all heard of a dental dam—that silly flap of latex that got its start in dentists' offices, but made its claim to fame spread across the beautiful beaver. But what a horrible name. Dental dam? I don't know about Dipstick, but I don't want anyone—no matter how hot she is—to use her teeth when going down on me, and I certainly don't want to remember the last root canal I had when I'm having sex. Couldn't they have come up with something better? How about cum curtain? Or sexy shade? Labia lingerie? Hoo hoo hoody?

Stupid name or not, dental dams are an important piece of latex. For example, if you use one, you won't get a case of raging herpes from that great pool player you met on Friday. Or how about genital warts? The woman from your poetry class—the one you're falling in love with, the one who read to you after you had sex—is carrying those. Dental dams, coming in all sorts of colors and flavors (do they have pussy flavor?), can prevent the transmission of these nasty sexually transmitted diseases, including HIV.

I know what you're thinking: I don't wanna use those dam things. They taste gross and they suck the intimacy out of a sexually charged moment. I agree, but wouldn't you rather have a box of dental dams drain the intimacy in lieu of the word "stop" as you're headed past her belly button?

Dealing with protection can be superawkward. When I first came out, I dated a woman who used to teach classes at a lesbian sex shop (yeah, lucky me). During the first month of our relationship, things were great—come to think of it, it only lasted a month (after you hear the story you'll understand why).

I was crazy about Julie. She was hot and sexy and we had such fun together—we hiked the Cascades, we shopped at Nordstrom's, we got pedicures side by side at the local spa. We were inseparable and even though we spent every minute together, we were taking it slow in the bedroom. When we hit the month benchmark, we decided it was time to take our relationship to the next level. So, we rented a beach cottage and planned a weekend getaway to commemorate the occasion.

It was a cold and misty night at the coast and after Julie lit a fire, she made her move on the couch. Taking the reigns, she lowered me and slowly worked her way down to my panty line. I was already in ecstasy. The beach house, the girl, the crackling logs. What could be better? Then suddenly, she asked me to hold on, saying she'd forgotten something. I smiled, wondering about what fun, delectable treat she had brought to pour on my body, a sticky something that she'd be lapping up for hours. Lying in wait, I nearly fell off the couch when she came back, snapping the rubber gloves onto her hands. "What are you doing with those?" I asked. "They're for protection," she said. Totally mortified, I lay back down and tried to enjoy myself.

We broke up shortly thereafter. Even though it was the dam-ish gloves that set me off, the root of our dysfunction merely surfaced in this event. We didn't communicate well (I think it was mostly me). At that moment, we should have discussed the gloves, then talked about the dental dam she brought out next. She knew I was a freshman and she should not have been so assuming. I, on the other (rubber-gloved) hand, should have been less of a pussy and spoken up about my discomfort, not just stared at the ceiling wondering why she thought I was dirty.

There are a lot of misconceptions about lesbian sex protection, yet there don't seem to be many clear answers, or at least readily accessible information for lesbians related to safe sex. What is and what isn't transferable during female oral sex? And how necessary are those dam things anyway if you're in a monogamous relationship? Don't let you and your honey get caught off guard. Latex can be good for a relationship. Even if you've already had sex and you've both only had a handful of partners, talk about protection today, before it becomes an itchy, red, enflamed problem . . . or worse.

DIPSTICK: Jeezus, Lipstick. I wish my first girlfriend worked in a sex store. I had to go through three women before I even had an orgasm. And pity the poor girls I was trying to please. I was eager, for sure, but beaver pleaser, I was not. Thank God my awkward teen years are over.

Sure, latex can suck, but it can also be a lifesaver. Even more important is to get yourself checked for sexually transmitted diseases. Don't think HIV is the only culprit. Fifty percent of sexually active women have human papillomavirus (HPV) and most don't even know it. HPV can show up as genital warts and can eventually lead to cervical cancer. Is that a gift you really want to pass on?

You work out at the gym, keep your hair and nails impeccably neat, and rub sunscreen on every time you go outside. It's time you treated your vagina and vulva with the same care. Make sure you get a pelvic exam. Regular gynecological care is as important as eating healthy, and good gynecological care will ensure healthy eating!

Lipstick: That was a good one, Dip.

DIPSTICK: I thought so.

But we're monogamous! Should we still practice safe sex?

Here's what Dipstick (and many other sex educators) recommends. For the first six months of your relationship during the Triple P, use a latex barrier every time you have sex. This includes condoms on sex toys.

After six months, you should both have Pap smears and STD blood tests. If you come back negative for STDs then you can stop using protective barriers.

However, if one of you has a viral STD like herpes, HIV, or hepatitis C then you need to continue to use latex barriers. If you have a bacterial infection like chlamydia, then use barriers until the infection is cleared up.

Wherever you stand, you'll have to decide what's best for your relationship, but the key, like Lipstick pointed out in the beginning, is good communication. Are we starting to sound like a broken record?

Where Can I Get a Headset for My Traveling Girlfriend?

Phone sex

"Humans are the only animals who can have sex over the phone."

—David Letterman

Lipstick: When Texas and I were first dating, we had great sex . . . about 1500 miles away from each other. It started out innocently, us musing about what we'd do to each together when she flew in for the weekend, and then slowly turned into something much more. Something hot and heavy that helped us get through those long, cold winter nights alone.

Eventually, when our phone sex reached epic proportions, I had to invest in some proper accoutrement. This became especially critical when the cordless phone I was using slid out of my sweaty hand and disappeared into the tub of water I was standing in. We were having sex by the "pool" at some elegant home on the cliff of Malibu on that particular evening. Texas didn't have access to a pool either, so she filled up her kitchen sink; I could hear her splashing about. After this little slip, I had to get a new phone, and guess what? It came with a frickin' headset. Perfect! Imagine all the fun I could have with *both* hands free. I'd never leave the house again!

In addition to having a wild imagination, there are a number of other tips I'd like to share.

Lipstick's phone sex tips

- Keep a roll of fresh batteries nearby.
- Drink a protein shake before you dial her digits.
- If you can score a wireless headset or if you're using a cordless phone, be sure you're on a different frequency than your neighbors. When I was young, the clock radio in my mom's bedroom once picked up a conversation my brother was having with his girlfriend years ago. I remember the look of horror on her face when she learned my brother, who was in high school at the time, was having sex—and she was simply trying to put on some ambient easy listening for her nap. (Note to those in the closet: Use landlines!)
- Be wildly creative. Jump in with both feet. Stretch both your limbs and your mind.
- Have "safe" sex. Give yourself and your lover the license to say whatever feels natural. Having a safe place free of judgment is essential to great phone sex. You gotta be able to roar like a tiger if you want, or, if the mood is right, tell her that you want to bend her over the chopping block and fuck her with a zucchini.

DIPSTICK: Roar like Tiger!? Lipstick, are you fantasizing about my wife again? Either way, you're so old-fashioned. Don't you know the computer keyboard has replaced the headset? Why do you think they call it IM— Instant Masturbation. Sure, you still need at least one hand to type, but lots of computers are coming with video cameras now so you can show off your goods while you virtually spank her bottom.

A few IM sex rules

- No sex at work. Even if you are on break.
- Be sure to empty your cache.
- Don't get lube on your keyboard.
- If you share a computer with your mother, be sure to delete those messages when you're done.

Phone sex, Internet sex, live-in-person sex, it's all good. We're just glad you're having sex. Get busy and stay busy!

Jean, Joan, and Me

Nonmonogamy

Lipstick: The thought of opening my relationship is so unappealing, it almost makes me nauseous. Yick! But, just because I'd rather stick a sharp pencil in my eye than let Texas ride another saddle, doesn't mean you can't have a successful polyamorous relationship.

But what is polyamory?

By definition, *polyamory* means participation in multiple and simultaneous loving or sexual relationships. Practically speaking, it means that you and/or your lover would have girlfriends on the side. And you'd know all about it; in fact, the two of you have worked out some agreed-upon "rules" governing this new arrangement. And the other girl(s) would certainly know about you, realizing and agreeing to enter into this polyamorous understanding.

Arrangements come in all shapes and sizes. Triads (three people involved in some way), quads, pentacles, sextets, and more! This is not all encompassing—there are many ways relationships are configured.

How do these relationships work?

Good question. Frankly speaking, I'm not sure. Lipstick's heart doesn't work this way and I've never been in a relationship that was nonmonogamous, nor has a girlfriend ever woken up, rolled over, and told me she wants to open our relationship (honey, don't get any ideas!). But I've met plenty of people who have made this arrangement work successfully. In fact, I hung out with a triad the other night.

A little background: I knew Marley and Maddy first. They'd been together for nearly ten years when they met Suzy. Prior to Suzy, they'd been in a monogamous relationship with an "openness" to it (they were open to sleeping with another person, as long as both were attracted and involved). Before Suzy, they'd slept with two other women.

I asked them how in the world that ever worked. The thought of Texas using the karaoke microphone on anyone else is repulsive.

"Neither of us have had problems with sexual jealousy," says Maddy.

Their secret?

You guessed it: *Communication!*

"We talk about everything, even if what we're feeling is irrational." Marley adds: "We always communicate in the moment . . . then we move on and don't hold onto it." Lipstick thinks this is sage advice.

Maddy had a crush on Suzy first, then, at a hot tub party, Marley realized she felt the same way. Before they knew it, they were in love—all of them. At the time of the interview, they'd been together for a year.

"We usually define our relationship as a triad," says Suzy. "We're still open to playing with other people."

Marley added: "It was really important for us at the beginning to have one-on-one dates. In reality, we don't just have one relationship with all three of us. Each of us has that relationship and also individual, unique relationships with the other two. Making sure that all of these relationships are strong was crucial."

When asked what problems arise in their arrangement, they're very honest and candid. For Suzy, the one who's new to the relationship, she says, "I feel like I have to overcompensate for not always being able to read Marley and Maddy. It can be really hard to see how they understand each other without having to talk and talk and talk . . . and I feel left out sometimes, not with time but with familiarity." Additionally, she says that since her relationship with them is fairly new, she gets lots of attention in the bedroom, which can cause intimacy problems for Marley and Maddy.

For Maddy, she struggles with not having as many common interests as Suzy and Marley, who enjoy gardening together and fucking in public (yes, you read that right).

"My worst enemy is time," says Marley, "and not having enough. Having two girlfriends, how do I divide my time?" she asks. (Beats Lipstick—I have a hard enough time keeping one woman happy!)

When it comes to nonmonogamy, Marley encourages people to break from the chains. "Don't let fear stop you from trying something new," says Marley. "You can open your heart to great love and your legs to fucking amazing sex and be the luckiest middle-aged woman alive!" she says.

Suzy says that no matter what your relationship looks like or how many people are involved, it's paramount to do it openly and truthfully: "It's all worth it in the end, even if it's hard in the beginning. Don't let society dictate who you are, who you love, or who you fuck."

Softie Warning!

If you're the supersensitive type who enjoys monogamous relationships and you meet some beautiful, polyamorous siren who you just can't help but fall for, beware. I've learned that rarely can you change the way your heart pumps blood based on circumstances. If you like having one honey at a time, someone who you can call your very own (me!), then I'd advise you not to dabble in this duality.

DIPSTICK: Like Lipstick, Dipstick, too, is wired to one lady, but that doesn't mean I didn't give polyamory a good shot. Well, really, I was just trying to be a good sport to my girlfriend at the time. See, she convinced young Dipstick that monogamy was just a patriarchal plot to keep women faithful to their husbands. She insisted sleeping with our roommate didn't lessen her feelings for me at all. Maybe so, but hearing their moans through the bedroom walls lessened a lot of things for me, like my self-esteem. And my mental health. The only thing not diminished that day was my blood pressure! As much as I tried to convince myself I was strong enough and evolved enough and feminist enough to handle polyamory, I just couldn't.

Now I know that strength, feminism, and evolution have nothing to do with it. She was a polyamorous being, set on convincing the world they should be like her. Dipstick won't do that. If you can make it work, more power to you and you and you . . .

Dry As a Bone

When your kitty won't play nice

Lipstick: Sometimes it seems that the pussy has a mind of its own. You're in bed with someone who you're wildly attracted to and when things get hot and heavy, little miss kitty decides she'd rather take a nap. There can be a number of reasons for kitty's lack of participation; the kooch has gotten pretty creative when it comes to how it gets out of sex. If you or your lover experience any of the dysfunctions outlined below, don't lose hope. Most, if not all, sexual disorders can be remedied with steadfast care or hard work. If you're not the one dealing, but your partner is having trouble, be patient and encourage her to see a doctor. In fact, it might be best for you to go

Lipstick & Dipstick's Sex Quiz: How Well Do You Know Lesbian Sex?

1. Tribadism is also known as:
    a. the flap.
    b. frottage.
    c. the triangle pose.
2. Polyamory means:
    a. fetish for polyester.
    b. fear of parrots.
    c. having multiple partners.
3. An erogenous zone is:
    a. a no parking zone.
    b. a sexually sensitive area.
    c. between your elbow and armpit.
4. Babeland is:
    a. a sex toy shop.
    b. a big lesbian circuit party.
    c. Melissa Etheridge's second album.
5. Which sex act is considered safe sex?
    a. kissing.
    b. unprotected oral sex.
    c. fisting.
6. The "D" in BDSM stands for:
    a. dildo.
    b. Dido.
    c. dominance.

with her, so you can have a better understanding of what you're dealing with. And no matter what, *never*, either consciously or unconsciously, make your partner feel badly about what's going on. As long as she's willing to seek help, be nothing but supportive.

Here are a few of the problems that plague lesbians:

Dry as a bone syndrome (a.k.a. female sexual arousal disorder). It's pretty clear what *dry as a bone* is, but I'll tell you anyway: it's when your pussy

7. Which sexually transmitted disease can lead to cancer?
      a. HIV/AIDS.
      b. HPV—human papillomavirus.
      c. herpes.
8. What is the world record for orgasms in one hour?
      a. 21.
      b. 134.
      c. 69.
9. A gold star is:
      a. a queer jean line.
      b. Olivia Cruise's newest ship.
      c. a dyke who's never been with a man.
10. If, after sex, there's a big wet spot in the middle of your mattress:
      a. your girlfriend wet the bed.
      b. someone ejaculated.
      c. you have a leaky roof.

   Correct Answers:
   1. b
   2. c
   3. b
   4. a
   5. a
   6. c
   7. b
   8. b
   9. c
  10. b

faucet is rusted shut. Your body refuses to produce natural lubrication and, sometimes, your clit simultaneously says "Nuh uh, I'm not swelling for you or anyone else."

Nobody's home disorder (a.k.a. anorgasmia). *Nobody's home* happens when the lights are off. When suffering, women can't reach orgasm through vaginal penetration or clitoral stimulation. Sexual desire makes no difference.

You could be dripping with desire for your lover, but when she goes down on you or straps on her third leg, you just can't quite get there. It reminds me of a time I was on the roller coaster at Six Flags. We were climbing to the highest plateau, the final drop before the ride was over, when—click, click, click—we stopped about four feet from the apex. For over an hour, we sat there looking at the sky wondering WTF, until finally, a voice came over a loud, hidden speaker. "Remain calm. The ride is broken," it said. And then a team of technicians helped us out of the cars and down a steep staircase to safety. Vaginas break down, too, and need a little help from our gyn-technicians. I was glad to get off the bunk ride, but I felt totally gypped and so should you if you can't taste the sweet, mind-boggling taste of orgasmic ecstasy. The causes for Nobody's Home include anger toward your lover, a lover that is lousy in bed (less common in the lesbian community because of home court advantage), religious baggage that discourages arousal (that sucks!), and shitty communication between you and your partner.

Hand me the remote syndrome—HMRS (a.k.a. inhibited sexual desire). Even though it's natural for your sex drive to diminish slowly over time, with HMRS the loss is persistent, almost cut off completely. The affects of HMRS are characterized by a lack of interest in poontang, but not just with your current partners—all together. You don't have fantasies, you don't masturbate, and you don't give a damn if there's a dirty movie on. You have zero libido and all you want to do is read trashy magazines and eat ice cream. Physical causes for HMRS vary from a hormonal imbalance, depression, and alcoholism to prescribed meds. Psychological causes include sexual trauma, relationship drama, stress in life or at work, and big shifts in life.

Kegelism (a.k.a vaginismus). For lesbians with kegelism, their vaginal door is practically closed. During penetration, or in the attempt at penetration, involuntary vaginal contractions make it almost impossible to get inside. If you're lucky, and you do get inside, it can be tremendously painful. There are a number of reasons why women suffer from kegelism. They include sexual or physical abuse, wherein kegelism is a phobic reaction to protect the vagina from penetration. Other causes run

the gamut—rape, religious baggage, fear that your pussy is too small
for whatever's knocking on its door, and pregnancy.

Yeouch-icardia (a.k.a dyspareunia). Yeouch-icardia is when your pussy
hurts like a motherfucker during sex, either during penetration or genital stimulation. The root of this scream in agony is either on the outside
or deep within the vagina. When a woman suffers from Yeouch-icardia,
she probably won't want to have sex at all, which often also leads to
HMRC and nobody's home syndrome. The usual suspects that cause
Yeouch-icardia are genital herpes, sexual trauma, inadequate lubrication, and a whole host of other medical causes.

The preceding is from Engenderhealth.org. For more information
about all of these sexual disorders, as well as appropriate treatment, consult
your gynecologist.

CHAPTER EIGHT

Dealing with the Unforeseen

DIPSTICK: "She did what!?!" Whatever it is, you didn't see it coming. Like being hit in the side of the head with a snowball, it stings and you're left with an uneasy feeling dripping down into your undergarments. But like that snowball, whatever your lover threw at you will eventually melt—or if it doesn't, you'll learn to love the snow.

Lipstick: Whaaaa . . . are you talking about?

DIPSTICK: OK, I'll put it this way: Life is either full of unexpected roadblocks, or challenging opportunities. It's all how you choose to look at it. With an open mind and open heart and a little guidance from Lipstick & Dipstick, you'll be working through life's surprises with the skill and grace of a figure skater.

Whether she wants to open the relationship or sleep with men, or you find out she's addicted to the Internet, it certainly wasn't what you signed up for when you executed the civil union contract.

Lipstick: That's more like it.

Carpal Cunthole Syndrome

Internet addiction

Lipstick: The Internet is a godsend. On it, we can find people we've lost touch with; we can find any tidbit of information with one or two Google searches; we can work in an almost paperless office; and we can find love—either through a dating service or cyber-sexing someone (who, btw, in reality, looks nothing like the woman in your fantasy). Beyond the goodness, the Internet also has a dark side; not only with scams and online predators, but Internet addiction is on the rise. If her Web surfing is getting in the way of your relationship then it's time to do something.

Five signs your partner might have an Internet addiction

1. The muscles in her forearm look like Popeye's. All those late-night double clicks have taken the place of her afternoon jogs.
2. She only responds when you call her by her IM handle.
3. During lovemaking, she gets of out of bed when she hears "You've got mail" from the other room.
4. She talks about her online friends like you talk about your childhood friends, and knows more about them than you know about your family.
5. When she does something she regrets, she says "Control Z."

DIPSTICK: Cute, Lipstick. The real signs of Internet addiction are a preoccupation with the Web, lying about how much time she spends online, a huge PayPal bill, and time on the Internet is interfering with other aspects of her life.

According to Kimberly S. Young, founder of the Center for Internet Addiction Recovery, there are several types of Internet addiction. Here are their lesbian counterparts:

Virtual sex party addiction: This is where your lady can't stop looking at sexy lesbian porn, or downloading the latest episode of *Sorority Sisters Gone Wild*. Your sex life will diminish because you can't live up to the copious amount of hotter, younger women out there.

My new best friends are windgrrl and butchmommie: This is where your sweetie engages in adultery with the person she thinks is a hot cop from Chicago, who is really a middle-aged overweight insurance salesman from Baton Rouge. Or she may not even be cheating, she may just have lots of chat room "friends" who quickly become more important than her real-life family and friends. (See section A Piece of HTML Pie.)

Cuntputer compulsion: She keeps playing that online game, or spends all your money on eBay. With a click of her mouse, your wedding savings are gone and pretty soon they're coming to repossess the car.

Just one more site addiction: With so much information out there, she can't help but click deeper and deeper into *L Word* fan sites, in search of any tiny tidbit of information she doesn't already have about Kate Moennig.

Solitaire can't stopitis: That new computer she got came equipped with so many cool games and she just can't stop playing them, hoping *this* time she will actually beat the computer.

Like any addiction, your partner must realize she has a problem before she can start on the road to recovery. You might want to check into an Al-Anon group. The good news is that, unlike drinking or drug addiction, your sweetie, once she gets her compulsive behavior under control, will be able to get online in small doses.

She has to want to change though—you can't make her. A good therapist can help. So can a 12-step group. One thing Dipstick does not recommend is a virtual support group. You tell her: Nice try, hon, but you're not going to fall for that.

Wanna Go to a Key Party?

Opening your relationship

Lipstick: Have you seen *The Ice Storm*, a great movie by Ang Lee? If you haven't, you might not know what a key party is. Essentially, a key party is a couple's swingers party where each pair who attends puts their car keys into a bowl at the door when they arrive. At the end of the night, one person from each couple goes to the bowl and pulls out a set of keys. Whichever person those belong to is who she goes home with.

I always get anxious when I watch this scene because I put myself in their shoes. The people who go to these parties must just be sex maniacs, interested in sexing any ole person. While a sex maniac, I, on the other hand, am superpicky about whom I shag. And, not only would I stand up with a fist when Texas was leaving with someone else, but I'd, no doubt, pick the ugliest person in the room, someone who I wasn't even interested in chatting with, let alone boinking! Thank god I don't live in a Hollywood movie.

But what happens before you get to the key party, or rather, open up your relationship? What happened earlier that week or that month when you girlfriend rolled over and said she's unhappy and wants to see other people?

If this happens to you, Lipstick encourages you to go see a therapist immediately. This is very tricky business, especially if one of you is against the idea. With the therapist you trust, you'll be able to get to the bottom of the conflict. Is she unhappy? Has she always had an appetite for others? Is it something she's tried to hide from you? Along with getting to the bottom of the issue, your therapist will also help you process and work through the discomfort and fear.

If you end up at the proverbial fish bowl digging out someone else's keys without getting professional help, don't be surprised if you're single in six months, and a little more jaded than before.

DIPSTICK: Oh, you're so dramatic, Lipstick. Different people have different sexual fantasies and some get really turned on by the idea of doing it with a stranger. There's nothing wrong with that.

Lipstick: Get your reading glasses out, Dip. I wasn't suggesting that there's anything wrong with having those fantasies or even acting on them. It can just be dangerous when you're in a relationship.

DIPSTICK: All right, well, what I do agree with is that both partners have to want it and lots of talks should happen beforehand. It doesn't mean that your relationship is falling apart.

I don't have personal experience in lesbian sex parties—I hear they're quite popular in San Francisco, but not NYC, not sure why (something about the "city that never sleeps around")—but I do know people who have opened up their relationship.

What I also know is if thousands of gay men can have open and anonymous sex, then I'm sure the three or four lesbians who want to try it can succeed.

Lipstick: That's like saying that just because a pack of dogs can pull a sled through Antarctica, so can a harem of short-haired domestic cats. You're wrong. Gay men and lesbians are *very* different animals capable and incapable of many things. Lesbos are Crock-Pots. Gay men are microwaves.

DIPSTICK: Be that as it may, I think there's a lot we can learn from our male counterparts. Here are some tips I picked up over the years from my boys.

Tips from gay men sex parties

- Never ask her name
- Certainly don't get her number
- If she asks for your name, give a fake one
- Always use protection
- If you go with your partner, let her choose who you want to do and never, I repeat, never bring the sex kitten home with you

Lipstick: Are we talking about sex parties or opening up your relationship?

DIPSTICK: Uh, you're the one who started talking about *The Ice Storm*.

Lipstick: Yeah, but I was just using it as an example.

Anyway, whether or not you've opened up your relationship sexually or have already stepped into Swingerville with your partner, please remember the most important things: (a) be sure the decision wasn't rooted in problems you're having at home, and (b) that you're both totally down with it. If you're not really clear on both these points, unfortunately, after your girl walks out the door with someone else's keys, she may never come back.

How to Get the Gag Out of Your Mouth

When your partner wants to explore S/M

DIPSTICK: My friend Yolanda was never interested in S/M, but after five years together, her girlfriend started to have S/M fantasies. Yolanda was uncomfortable, but decided to try it anyway to please her partner. Was she ever sorry! Once she said yes the first time, she was never able to say no again. Pat pressured her. For a year, Yolanda dreaded sex, always wishing that Pat would get over her obsession.

Some girls are totally turned on by whips and chains and others are totally turned off. I don't think you can make yourself want to be flogged or get wet at the thought of cutting into your lover's tender breasts.

If you are turned on by your lover's fantasies, or at the very least curious, then by all means give it a go, but don't do anything you're not comfortable with. Dipstick can't stress this enough.

Lipstick: Yolanda should have been honest with Pat from the get-go. She played a role—even if it was tied up to a medieval bedpost—in the demise of their relationship.

DIPSTICK: You're right, she should have stood up for herself after she realized she didn't like rough sex. I know another couple who ran into a similar snag. After ten years together, Amy's partner Mary decided she wanted to explore "power over" sex—her fantasy was to be a dominatrix. A survivor of sexual abuse, Amy had no desire to go there. She didn't want to give up ten years with Mary either. So, they decided Mary could be free to explore her desires outside of the relationship. Mary found blonde bombshell Ryan through a personal ad and the sex was good, but being lesbians, Mary and Ryan fell in love. To this day, Mary is involved with both Amy and Ryan. They have an open relationship and it works for them. Sure, they have issues, but what relationship doesn't?

Lipstick: If I was into S/M, no doubt I'd be a sadist. I like to tell people what to do—hence, I'm an irreverent advice columnist—and kinky sex turns me on.

If your partner comes home one day with a leash and a crotchless teddy for you to wear, you'd best indulge her fantasy. In fact, that's always a good rule of thumb, as long as it doesn't cause you or anyone else harm. And only if it's not too creepy. If you're not sure whether what she wants you to do is OK, shoot me an e-mail and I'll be the judge. With my whip in hand, I promise to be painfully honest. Crack.

If your lover's request passes Lipstick's litmus test, and your first inclination is to still say "no way!" then I'd encourage you to work on your self-esteem. I believe that cowardice and discomfort in the bedroom are directly related to one's self-confidence. If you want to be better in bed, then work on the inside first. Now, being tied up and cracked with a whip might not be your idea of a good time—in fact, maybe you'd rather have diarrhea in a crowded public bathroom than get in that damn swing again—but at least you've satisfied your partner. A great sex life is all about communication and experimentation, with a pinch of compromise. It's all about bending for your partner, even if that means bending over the yoga ball while she bounces you around the room.

After you've cooperated in your partner's favorite fantasy, you, nipple clamps and all, need to let your girl know that the ball gag makes you feel claustrophobic, or whatever your gripe is. Communicate! Compromise and come up with what works for both of you—something that satisfies her insatiable appetite to tie you up but doesn't exceed your tolerance for pain.

Pussy Nervosa (a.k.a. Julie Cypher Syndrome)

When she wakes up attracted to men

DIPSTICK: I believe sexuality is fluid. Especially for women. Why else would so many ladies come out in their forties and so many hard-core dykes fall for men. If you're one of the unlucky ones whose partner wakes up and decides she's straight, Dipstick feels for you. This very thing happened to my friend Joanna. Literally. Her girlfriend woke up one morning and said she wanted to date men. Joanna was floored. After all, Kristy had been a lesbian all her life.

"She slept with Melissa Etheridge for Christ's sake!" Joanna cried to me on the phone.

What can you do? Sorry ladies, but the only option is to kiss her goodbye. Give her some condoms as a farewell gift.

Lipstick: I'm gonna bet that nine times out of ten, the partner who gets dumped for a penis saw the big head coming from a mile away. Whether or not the girl had ever confessed to being bisexual, you probably always knew she was. I believe there are a lot of closeted bisexuals out there claiming to be lesbians. There are two reasons these dick lovers hide their true identity: first, the negative stigma associated with the word *bisexual*. Some women are afraid to identify for fear of being chastised, and in some social circles, I'd imagine, it's grounds for the boot. So, they end up hiding their true selves, which only festers, and when the relationship is finally over and they step out with a man (which is just like most lesbians who have someone on the side before they break up with their lovers), they become these lesbian-hated icons. Remember how much we hated Anne Heche for what she did to Ellen? The second reason why this happens is that many dykes are cynical and bitter. At some point in their lesbian path, they foolishly fell for a straight woman who broke their heart, so they're totally adverse—almost repulsively so—to women who're bisexual. It's a gag reflex.

DIPSTICK: Lipstick, I think you should stop theorizing on WHY some girls go to guys and start helping out the poor girl who was just dumped for a dildo substitute. And I think you're giving bisexuals a bad name. Truth is, most bisexuals have no problem making a commitment to one person. Just because they like both sexes, doesn't mean they can't settle for one.

Lipstick: Give me a break. How am I giving bisexuals a bad name? I love bisexuals and I'm not saying they can't commit. Where you're wrong, Dip, is that it's important to understand all sides of an issue when dealing with a breakup, especially what is at its source. Dykes need to understand that these women aren't leaving them because they suck in bed or are emotionally inept—although both reasons may have played a role, depending on the lesbian—but that the writing may have been on the wall in the months or years leading up to the phallic declaration. They may have been in denial that their relationship was falling apart.

DIPSTICK: 'K, whatever. Girls, when your lover decides she's fallen for a man, or wants to try to bag one, it can be harsh, but really, it's no different than your lover waking up one day and telling you she is no longer in love with you and is leaving you for her kayak teacher. Yes, it hurts. Yes, it sucks. Yes, you need support. Fortunately for you, there are plenty of angry lesbians like Lipstick who will give it to you.

Lipstick: Are we even on the same planet, Dipstick? I'm so misunderstood.

DIPSTICK: Seriously, it's going to be hard, but look on the bright side. At least you won't see her and her new catch making out in a dark corner of the lesbian bar. She's one ex you probably won't have to avoid at Gay Pride next year.

Balls to the Wall

When she wakes up and wants to be a man

Lipstick: As the transgender movement continues to gain momentum, more people are comfortable facing their demons—that nagging insistence that's haunted them their whole lives telling them they were born in the wrong body. What does this mean? It means waking up and discovering that your girl wants to be a boy (female to male or FTM) could actually happen to you, especially if you date butch babes.

DIPSTICK: Hold on there, Lipstick. Sure the butch may be a dying breed but don't scare the sisters away from us. We're not ALL turning into men. It is still much more likely that you'll be hit by a drag queen driving a bus while crossing Castro than your partner waking up a man.

Lipstick: Queens in buses aside, there are three very important things to keep in mind if this happens to you.

The first thing to do, after you freak the fuck out, is to let your partner know you love her/him unconditionally. Seriously. Put your selfish feeling of abandonment and your own identity crisis—will I still be a dyke?—aside. Remember when you came out of the closet? Remember how important it was to know you were in a safe place.

Second, pick up the phone and call a good therapist. This animal is far too big to slay alone. Find a couples therapist—preferably one that specializes in transgender people and sexual identity issues.

Last, be loyal to your partner and be there for her/him as a friend.

DIPSTICK: Fourth, get yourself a support group. This is going to be a long process, and according to psychologists who specialize in trans issues, a necessarily selfish one for the trans person.

Your previously attentive partner has a lot of soul searching to do. She/he may be your main support, or she/he may be so caught up in her/his own process that she/he is unable to relate to what you're going through.

Some issues you may encounter as a partner of a trans person:

Money. If your partner decides to physically alter her/his body, that surgery is going to cost you both. Most insurance companies don't cover it. Your partner may feel having surgery is an absolute necessity, whereas you wanted that chunk of change to go toward a new MINI Cooper.

Dealing with the medical issues. If your partner has top or bottom surgery, she/he is going to be laid up for some time and will need you to take care while she/he recovers. You may have to spend your vacation time tending to a bandaged and bloody chest: removed breasts you were sad to say good-bye to.

A big move. If you live in a rural area, you may decide that the only safe way to transition is to move to a city. Losing your friends and support system at this time when you need it the most can be the thing that makes or breaks a relationship. No matter where you live, be sure to get support for yourself. The Internet can be a great resource for this sort of thing. Try Transfamily at transfamily.org. Another good resource is *Trans Forming Families: Real Stories About Transgendered Loved Ones* by Mary Boenke.

Now he's a gay man. No one knows why, but a percentage of FTMs surprise themselves—not only do they become men, but now they're attracted to them. Loren Cameron, author of *Body Alchemy: Transsexual Portraits* says, "A funny thing happened to me on my way to becoming a man . . . I began to want one." Don't be surprised if your new man suddenly has an urge, not just to have a penis, but to suck one.

She Talks to Her Softball Coach Seventeen Times a Day

Emotional cheating

Lipstick: The sin of all relationship sins—well, at least the biggest one short of screwing your softball coach behind the bleachers—is emotional cheating. A warm, psychological heart fuck is just as damaging as actually strapping on a big schlong or heading face-first into her furry catcher's mitt.

But what is an emotional affair or a heart fuck?

That's a good question, one that doesn't have a firm *Webster's* answer. A heart fuck is like intuition, or the girl of your dreams: you can't articulate it, but you know it when you see it or feel it.

If there's one thing that really gets me fired up, it's when people say emotional cheating doesn't exist. I think this type of psychosomatic stepping out is the seed—no, the spawn—of the relationship devil itself: adultery. (Small caveat: why is it called *adultery*? I think it should be called *adolescentry*; by the time you're an adult, you should know better and have control over your horny paws.)

Those of you who say emotional cheating is harmless or isn't real are in denial. What do you call those eleven phone calls you put into your coworker while she was out of town? How about those long hours you spoke to that new friend in your science class? The e-mails you try to hide from your girlfriend? Sure, you haven't actually touched anyone else ... yet. Well at least not in a way that would constitute cheating, you justify. If you're still insistent you've never been an emotional cheater or never seen it before, here are some ways to identify heart fucking:

Shady business. Everything you do surrounding this new "friend" is fishy, even to you. Will the real Slim Shady please stand up? Go ahead and get your ass out of that chair! You guard your inbox like a prison guard and you find yourself lying for no reason when it comes to things that relate to this friend. You may (and that's a small *may*) tell your honey you spoke, but you certainly won't tell her it was nine times ... before lunch, not including the three e-mails you exchanged that morning. Sometimes your shady business surprises even you. All of a sudden one day it creeps up and you automatically lie or dodge questions. By this time, it may be too late to stop the actual wound caused by emotional cheating, but it's never too late to stop the bleeding, especially if your girlfriend doesn't know. Usually she does. Women are quite intuitive.

That little voice. Your heart whispers, "Don't do this," but you're so deep in denial you block it out. You've somehow convinced yourself that what you're doing is innocent and playful. You're in a relationship and you love your girlfriend. There's no harm. Think again. And listen to that little voice in the back of your mind telling you it's a bad idea to tell that friend if she were single you'd ask her out. That loaded flattery will only cause trouble.

DIPSTICK: Well, I'm gonna get your G-string in a bunch, Lipstick, because I call foul on this emotional cheating business. Here's an example of why I don't think it exists.

When my Tiger decided to run a marathon, she and her good friend Candace started training together. They would go on long runs four or five times a week and talk on the phone every other day. When they weren't running and talking, they were checking in with each other via e-mail. One morning the wife turned to me and told me about a dream she had just had. After completing a challenging, but stunning run, Candace turned to her, pulled off her Dri-FIT top and running bra, and proceeded to lick the sweat off her areola. I rolled back over, hugged my pillow, and said, "That's nice, honey," before falling back to sleep.

See, to Dipstick, if it doesn't happen in real time, then it's not cheating. She can fantasize, dream, and even flirt with another woman. Unless there's skin contact involved, it's not cheating.

Everyone gets crushes on other people. Tell me you and your lover don't have a "celebrity exception" rule. If Leisha Hailey wants to sleep with her, then she can, and it's agreed that it's OK. Here are the five I'm allowed to shag should the opportunity arise:

1. Jennifer Beals
2. Alicia Keyes
3. Gwen Stefani
4. Pink
5. Frances McDormand

We also get crushes on regular people. Tiger knows I have a long-standing crush on an old music festival buddy. You could have a crush on a new partner at work, your vet, or that cute barista at the Starbucks down the block. Crushes on therapists and personal trainers don't even count. Hell, I think it's a requirement.

Crushes make life exciting. When someone thinks you're hot, you start to feel hot. Your lover will bring that spark home, both to the bedroom and the rest of your relationship. So, if you trust her, don't worry about it. It's not cheating unless the other woman touches your skin in a sexual manner.

Lipstick: As usual, you totally missed the boat, Dipstick. Like I said before, I don't think fantasizing, having a sexual dream, or crushing out on someone else is cheating. That's absurd. I, too, think it's healthy to talk about stuff like that—in fact, Texas had a dream about Sigourney Weaver the other night and was pissed my alarm clock tore her out of the hot moment. I just smiled, slid on my slippers, and went downstairs to make the coffee, hoping she could pick up where she left off.

I certainly don't think crushes are harmful. I get crushes all the time. They're fun.

All of this is far different from emotional cheating. It's when you take these crushes and act on them that is taboo—everything to the point of actually touching the other person. You know what I'm talking about, intuitive readers, and just because Dipstick doesn't get it, doesn't mean there aren't legions of you out there who do. Anyone who's been cheated on emotionally understands it all too well.

Here are the five I can shag:

1. Jennifer Beals
2. Kate Winslet
3. Scarlett Johansson
4. Susan Sarandon
5. Diane Lane

Whether you know what I'm talking about or not (you do!), odds are you've done some things regarding a certain someone else you want to keep under wraps. Be careful when you hear those little voices—they're speaking for a reason!

How Could I Be in Love with Her?

Falling for the best friend

DIPSTICK: Our relationships with our best friends are way less complicated than those with our lovers. There's none of the baggage, the expectations are different, and usually you're having a good time together. It's perfectly natural to have feelings for your best friend. You might even get drunk, make out, and profess your love for each other.

This is no problem, unless, of course, you're in a monogamous relationship with someone else. Then it's just plain ole cheating.

Lipstick: Whoa, whoa, whoa. Relationships with best friends can be just as complicated as romantic relationships—in fact, sometimes, even more so.

And especially in the dyke community. The line between friend and lover has never been so thin, so gray, than where it cuts through in a platonic lesbian friendship.

DIPSTICK: Plutonic? Is that a relationship on Pluto?

Lipstick: Oops, platonic.

DIPSTICK: I dated a gal years ago. Sheila and her buddies used to go off to Provincetown every Memorial Weekend, while Dipstick headed off to the women's music festival. One year, I came back all happy to see her, but Sheila was looking glum and guilty. Turns out, she had slept with her best friend in P-town. She came back crying, saying she was sorry, but wasn't sure how it happened, and didn't understand how she'd woken up one day and found herself in love. I was furious and sent Sheila packing. I actually still get fired up about it. In fact, right now, my neck is bright red.

Lipstick: Dipstick, you need to let that anger go and try to get back on the horse. I say yes lesbians can be best friends platonically, but only if they take good care of the line and respect it, especially when you're in another relationship.

DIPSTICK: The point I'm trying to make is that lesbians do occasionally fall for their best friends. As a matter of fact, this scenario is so common it's become cliché in lesbian novels and films. When it happens to two "straight" ladies we cheer from the audience, but when it's two dykes, one or both of who are in a relationship, it can make even the strongest butch cry.

If you find yourself falling for your best friend, there are several things you can do:

- Dive into your girlfriend's pants and don't come out for three weeks.
- Change your home phone number, your cell phone, your IM account, your e-mail address, and the locks on your door.
- Be mature and have a heart-to-heart with your friend. The only way to work things out is through honest conversation. She's your best friend; after all, if you can't trust her, who can you trust?

Lipstick: Did I hear you right, Dipstick? Talk to her about it? That's crazy. Don't open up about it; that will only fuel the fire. Instead, pull away, get a grip on your emotions, and refocus on your girlfriend. We all get crushes, but we all don't need to be cheaters.

Here's an especially dangerous scenario to look out for:

Fast friends. You know when you meet someone and you click immediately? You wonder how you ever survived without her and imagining life before her is impossible. This is all fine and good as long as you—all together now, girls—*respect the line*. You should fully embrace your friends and your friendships, but just be forewarned that sometimes these friendships are budding love affairs. If you're both dykes and there's even a twinge of attraction between you two, *beware*. Like so many lezbots before you, you could fall into the love trap. You're actually having a love affair sans sex, until—wham!—it catches up with you late one night while you're talking and the next thing you know you've turned a corner and are suddenly grinding on the couch.

DIPSTICK: This would never happen with butch best buddies. Here's how Dipstick says to avoid the whole thing:

- Only befriend straight women.
- Only befriend men.
- If you fall for femmes only, then befriend butches.
- Butches can be friends with anyone, because we all know butches never cheat.

Lipstick: Hey there, Nut Case, aren't you late to meet your friends from the garage at Joe's Tavern? I've seen you there lined up with your guy friends, drinking beer, and shifting your "balls."

Here are some *real* tips to keep your friendship on the right track:

- Don't sleep together.
- Don't have sex.
- Don't make out.
- No holding hands after sunset.
- No spooning.

If you don't follow the five steps above, you might get in over your head and find yourself suddenly in love with your BF. Most lesbians respect the line because they've been burned by it in the past—either as the one who crosses it or the one whose current girlfriend did.

DIPSTICK: If you've tried everything and you just can't stay away, just can't keep your hands off your BF, then it's time for you to make the tough decision. Leave your girl, start shacking up with Buffy, and pray it's the right decision.

A Piece of HTML Pie

Internet cheating

Molly and Renee were together for five years when Molly discovered Renee was having e-mail conversations with different women from all over the world. Although the e-mails were sexual and suggestive, Renee could not understand why Molly was upset. "It's not an affair! I've never met these women!" she shouted. Molly was especially distressed to learn that Renee was using some of the same language she used with her when they were in the bedroom. It sickened her to think of it.

Lipstick: I bet Renee didn't show Molly those sexual e-mails or the IM print out of the cybersex she had with Big Boobs in Birmingham. I bet Molly found them!

DIPSTICK: Yep, I bet you're right. Like we said regarding Internet addiction, the World Wide Web can be such an amazing tool. It can bring the world into our house with a few keystrokes. It's a perfect place to have all your fantasies come true. People don't have to be honest about anything. You can make yourself rich, tall, and a world traveler. You can meet someone you think is from Thailand, but is really in Toledo. She can say she's a lawyer, when really she sits at home all day watching *Judge Judy*.

And because of the anonymity, you can share those sexual fantasies with your online buddies that you might be afraid to share with a partner. Dipstick has never been one for Internet sex or phone sex, but the appeal is apparent. The question is: Is it cheating?

Dipstick says it's only cheating if skin touches skin. Chatting dirty online with some hussy from Hoboken is no worse than reading and writing erotica. I encourage lesbians to explore their sexual selves. What I typically see is too much sexual repression in the lesbian community.

Lipstick: Hold on. Dipstick, you honestly believe your girlfriend cybersexing some woman across the pond isn't cheating? You must be one of those virtual hoochy poos to be living behind such a justified veil. You've internally negotiated this one, huh, Dip?

DIPSTICK: I'm not having Internet sex with anyone, I'm just saying that there's too much repression in the dyke community so women should be free to type and masturbate away. How is it any different than porno—if you're never going to meet the person?

Lipstick: Well, I disagree. Lipstick believes that if you're doing anything you wouldn't want your girlfriend to find out about, you're guilty and you know it.

I've had Internet sex and it's not all bad—it's like those interactive video games you play on Xbox, only with more imagination and a big bang at the end. When Texas and I were dating long distance, and we weren't having phone sex (which I think is much more fun and it's easier to hold the sex toys, especially if you get a headset, remember?), we tried out cybersex.

In fact, I got busted for having a dirty little chat with my girlfriend at work. I know, it was irresponsible and immature, but it was on my lunch hour, I hated my job and missed her so much. Besides, who knew Big Brother was reading my AOL mail! Isn't there something illegal about that?

DIPSTICK: I think there is!

Lipstick: Anyway, what I was doing wasn't cheating, but if it was with someone besides Texas, it would've been. The Internet has opened up a whole new can of worms. Even if you are cheating, how are you to know the 5'9" blonde from the Bay Area isn't some middle-aged guy in his basement? The scary thing is you don't. Wouldn't it suck to ruin your relationship for some dude that works the Circle K night shift?

The bigger issue, of course, is the fact that you're cheating on your girlfriend. If you're thinking about some chick you "finger-banged" (or is that findfger-bang$^@ed :-P) the night before online, then you're not present and it handicaps your relationship. What aren't you getting from her that you're able to get with a mouse and an LCD screen? If you find yourself trolling for women to "talk" to, this is a huge red flag. Something's wrong at home.

DIPSTICK: Sure trolling for women to talk to is wrong. That implies emotional connection. But I still contend that cybersex is no different than cyber porn, it's just a little more interactive.

Lipstick: Hmmm. Still not with ya, Dip. If you're in a relationship, wrap a tourniquet—a.k.a. emotional responsibility and respectful restraint— around your keyboard and sign off, no matter how much you dream of cyber-Lolita's fingers tapping the keys. Like you rationalized in the beginning, I've heard many people say it's not cheating if it's not physical, blahsy blah. Hogwash! The virtual world can be dangerous. Not only can your computer catch viruses, but if you put yourself in the wrong places—for example, single lesbian chat rooms—your relationship can, too.

The Out-of-Town Rule

Opening your relationship when out of town

DIPSTICK: The out-of-town rule is when one of you is out of town, you can have an affair, as long as you never see this person again and what happens out of town stays out of town.

Some couples, especially those where one partner is on the road a lot, agree to this setup. It's an open relationship with very specific boundaries. Dipstick thinks this could work very well, although she has never tried. How cool would it be to meet some hot girl at a conference and make out with her in her hotel room with no guilt and no commitments?

Lipstick: You're really starting to sound like a guy.

DIPSTICK: There are variations on the out-of-town rule. In some cases, only making out is allowed. In others, you can go all the way, as long as you use protection. (See section Get Out of My Dam Bed.)

If you are one of those lesbians who travels a lot for work, talk to your partner about this, but not the night before you leave. Or worse, from the hotel pay phone, while the hottie is in your room and ready to go!

If only one of you travels and the other is at home, she might get jealous and think it's unfair that you get to mack on beautiful women, while she is left to clean out the litter box and sort your mail. If this is the case, you might need to send her out of town from time to time on make-out vacations.

Lipstick: I'm not sure what planet you're living on, Dipstick, but down here in the real world, the lesbians and I have a message for you: *You're fucking crazy.*

Sure, this may indeed be how some lesbian couples do it when one of them travels a lot, but the only reason it works is because the one at home doesn't know about the arrangement. Dykes just can't do this. Women aren't programmed this way. We are like swans; we're very monogamous. Of course, with everything, there are exceptions—women who can have open relationships or make polyamory work—but now I'm wondering if they're actually from the same place as you, Dip: Planet Poontang. (That was said with love for my poly friends!)

DIPSTICK: Say whatever you want, Lipstick, but my feet are planted right here on the earth.

Lipstick: I do believe "What happens in Vegas, stays in Vegas," but I just can't see how women can fool around on the road and leave it there. Maybe I need some schooling, or an intensive detachment workshop from Texas. While it would be fun—oh so fun—to make out with some Mistress in Manhattan, here are ten things I'd rather do than find out my wife had the mistress:

1. Shove a fork in my eye.
2. Drink Windex.
3. Eat nothing but Rocky Mountain oysters for the rest of my life.
4. Have an allergic reaction to lube.
5. Join the Church of Scientology.
6. Watch Fox News.
7. Be dragged behind a semi truck.
8. Have a colonoscopy.
9. Give Rush Limbaugh a Brazilian wax.
10. Chew my arm off at the elbow.

DIPSTICK: What's a Brazilian wax?

Lipstick: You and your big bush don't want to know. It will give you nightmares.

OPP—Other People's Pussy

When you cheat

DIPSTICK: I'm a terrible liar. Whenever I try to tell a lie, my face turns red, I smirk, and I flub what I'm saying. Thank God I'm not a cheater, because I would be so busted!

Dipstick never advocates lying, even if you have committed the heinous lesbian crime of cheating on your partner. The one time I was out of town and away from my sweet Tigress (we hadn't been dating too long) and my lips accidentally ran into another girl's, I had to confess. Right away. I don't mean I called her and let her fret and worry at home, but as soon as she picked me up from the airport, I came clean.

It's true, she was pissed, and I didn't get my typical homecoming sex that night, but I didn't deserve it, did I? Eventually she forgave me, when I promised it would never happen again. And it hasn't!

What if I had lied and she found out about it later? She would never have trusted me again. If you slip up and accidentally fall face first into another girl's panties, fess up! It will be hard and it won't be pretty, but at least you'll have a chance to repair your relationship.

Lipstick: Was that when we were at the white party in Palm Springs and got separated? I didn't mention it, but you had lipstick all over your white shirt when I found you later that night. You said you were "listening to music" in the other room?

I've never cheated on my wife or a girlfriend, so I can only put myself in the cheated-on shoes, which I've worn before. They're a painful pair of heels with two razor blades that hold your toes—and heart—into place. (I've also kinda been the other woman, but that's another story—maybe for our next book.)

DIPSTICK: What do you mean "kinda?" This is a story even I haven't heard yet!

Lipstick: If Texas cheated on me, I'd absolutely want to know right away. Here are the reasons: The first is respect. No matter how measly, it shows that she respects me enough not to make me the fool. And even though I'd be devastated, I'd still have an ounce (maybe a half-ounce) of respect left for her because she'd had the courage to tell the truth, not knowing what my reaction would be. Second, if she did cheat, I'd want to understand why she was unhappy and what was lacking in our relationship. Unless they're compulsive, people don't cheat for no reason. Third, I'd want to have the opportunity to deal with it. Whether or not we could bounce back, I'm not sure. I don't know how I'd react. Would we see a therapist? I'd hope that by that time, we'd have already been in therapy. Would I stay? Would I leave? Just go away for awhile? These are all questions I don't have answers for; questions I couldn't possibly answer until I'm in the heat of the moment.

There are times when I wouldn't want to know. Dipstick touched on one of them. If she's out of town, she'd best get her ass home first before she drops the bomb. I'd also prefer not to know if it happened years ago. I would instantly lose so much respect for her that I'm not sure we could recover. What else had she hidden over the years? Once trust is gone, it is hard to get it back, but once respect is gone, forget it!

There's nothing worse than finding out you've been cheated on. Double D cheated on me so many times I lost count. Is it cheating if you're in the closet and it's with a guy? It sure felt like it did.

DIPSTICK: Yes, Lip, it counts. Anytime your heart is involved in a monogamous relationship.

Lipstick: But we had these fucked up rules that we could go on dates. She just decided to make out with a couple of them.

DIPSTICK: I say she still cheated.

Lipstick: Well, I'll be sure to throw a pack of gum at her or something much less damaging next time we get together for dinner.

DIPSTICK: Just as long as it's not a pack of cigarettes, I know she's trying to quit.

Lipstick: One final thought I'd like to add is that I'd much rather Texas Two-Step come clean about an affair and we deal with the aftermath than for her to live with the insidious guilt for years. I love her too much. I'd be mad as hell, and I can't say our relationship would make it out alive, but if she carries that deep secret around, she probably won't survive long either. Keeping dark secrets in corners of your soul is cancerous and it will eat you from the inside out. Fess up.

CHAPTER NINE

Thin Ice

All right, so things aren't going quite as planned. You know you love her, but lately you just haven't been *feeling* it. Don't panic. Every relationship has trouble from time to time. It's how we get through these rocky times that really speaks to the staying power of our relationships.

In the next few sections, Lipstick & Dipstick will guide you through those really tough times. The times when you just want to pull your hair out—or worse, hers. We'll help you figure out which relationships are worth saving and which ones you just need to dump. And we'll definitely tell you what *not* to do when your relationship is falling apart. Climb on board. It will be a bumpy ride, but we'll get you there safely.

Line of Fire

Tempting situations

DIPSTICK: I love the Temptations! That song "My Girl" should be on every lesbian's play list. But if there's trouble at home, you should avoid the temptations. An alcoholic doesn't have Bacardi in the fridge and if you're having issues with your girl, don't go out drinking with the cute new intern at your office.

Lipstick: Sometimes you know when temptation is coming. Other times it sneaks up on you when you least expect it, only realizing it when your hand's already unsnapping the intern's bra. At all costs, no matter how enticing, steer clear of tempting situations when you and your girlfriend are having problems. In case you're clueless, here's a basic advisory system to help you gauge what you should do.

Lesbian Relationship Security Advisory System

Code Green. This is when you're thrown into a situation where your girlfriend is absent and . . . there are other lesbians around.

What to do: Have a smokin' good time and cut a rug.

Code Blue. There are other lesbians around and you and your partner are having problems.

What to do: Go out, have a great time, but be home at a reasonable hour.

Code Yellow. There are sexy dykes around, including several you have a crush on, there's alcohol involved, and you and your partner are having problems.

What to do: Proceed with caution and when on the dance floor, keep your hands to yourself. Three drinks max. Be home by midnight.

Code Orange. There are many, many attractive lesbians, as well as one in particular you've been crushed out on for a long time. There's unlimited alcohol, it's summertime, and the problems you and your girlfriend are having stem from the fact you haven't had sex in over a year.

What to do: Watch the fuck out! Be on your best behavior and remember you're in a relationship. One drink max. Be home by 11:00 P.M.

Code Red. There are so many hot lesbians, you think you've died and gone to heaven. This includes that sexy friend of yours who you've become especially close to recently. You've both admitted that attraction. The two of you almost kissed once before, but fortunately your cell phone rang and interrupted the moment. You've opened up to her about you and your partner's lack of sex and she's empathized. There's unlimited alcohol, it is summer, and you're at a pool party. Tops are coming off and your girlfriend is out of the country.

What to do: Turn around, go home, lock the doors, and close the blinds. Masturbate, have several orgasms if you can. Do not leave the house or answer the door for any reason.

This advisory system is to help you make better choices. I'm thinking about having them put on pocket-size laminated cards for your easy reference, as well as shrunk down even smaller so they can fit in your bikini top or jog bra. Stay tuned.

DIPSTICK: That's a great idea, Lip. Maybe we could post them at the entrance of every lesbian bar in the country, too.

Lipstick: Totally. If you don't use this handy advisory system to gauge circumstantial temptation, then I'd advise you to use your head. You know that little trigger in your body that's responsible for flight or fright, injecting your body with adrenalin so you can get away from danger? Train yourself to flip that switch when you get in over your head with another woman, so you can run like hell.

Should I Stay or Should I Go?

How to know if what you have is worth saving

Lipstick: In our relationships, we often come to a crossroad, where we have to decide which way to proceed. It could be that someone was unfaithful, that a job was taken in another city, or that one of you decides she was born in the wrong body and wants to transition. Whatever the reason, you have a decision to make—should you stay together or split up? When faced with this question, let intuition guide you.

DIPSTICK: My intuition got me into a lot of trouble once. I thought my girlfriend was cheating and I followed her around one rainy afternoon. Turns out she was just trying to plan a surprise party for me.

Every relationship falls on hard times: she had an affair, racked up her third DUI, or you're just not having sex anymore. How do you determine whether it's time to leave? This simple list oughta help.

You should stay if:

- she supports you financially.
- she has a hot body and the sex is good.
- she is rich and old and about to die.

- you work for her daddy.
- she's pregnant.

You should go if:

- she tells you she's in love with your mother.
- she tells you she's in love with your brother.
- she emptied your bank account and now has your credit card.
- she's still got ten left on a fifteen-year sentence.
- she's unemployed and never gets out of her PJs.

Lipstick: You're funny, Dip. Here are some things to consider:

Can't seem to break that jealous pattern, where she sometimes embarrasses you in public? It might be time to say good-bye.

Do you love the way she takes care of you and is committed to working on her shortcomings, even though they continue to persist? It might be a good idea to wait it out and see what happens.

Did she forget your birthday last year and accidentally forget to feed your cat while you were in Rome? Perhaps she should go.

Does she call you at work just to say she loves you, even though her unemployed, lazy ass was still in bed when you left at dawn? Maybe you just need to prod her and tell her you believe in her dreams.

She hasn't cleaned the house since you moved in together even though you've asked her a million times to help with chores? It might be time to put her out with the recycling.

Does she have her heart set on acreage in the country and you like the condo in the city? Even though I hate the suburbs, maybe you could compromise on something in between?

You've got to trust your intuition and ask yourself these hard questions when it comes down to these big decisions. Do you see yourself growing old together? Are you committed to working through whatever is troubling your relationship? Will she ever buy you that ring you want from Tiffany's?

Be honest and trust your gut. It will never steer you wrong.

Hail to the Couples Counselor

Getting help

DIPSTICK: I have a friend who swears that seeing a couples counselor is the kiss of death for any relationship. Dipstick disagrees. Every relationship hits a rough patch, and many lesbians I know reach a critical point at year five. That's when Dip and Tiger went to see the couples counselor.

I won't get into the details, but let's just say things were not looking good for the future of our relationship. We were arguing all the time, unhappy, stifled, and not having sex. We needed help and we needed it fast. Thank God for the sweet woman our chiropractor recommended. In just six short sessions, we ironed out the kinks and have been rock steady ever since. All right, not rock steady—we've still had a few rocky times—but we've never gotten to the point where we actually contemplated *leaving* again.

Making the decision to see a counselor is a hard one. Admitting that you need outside help to deal with a very personal problem can make you feel like your life is out of control. If you were failing out of college, you wouldn't hesitate to hire a tutor, right? If you wanted to run a triathlon, you'd hire a personal trainer. If you wanted to start your own business, you'd hire a business coach. Seeing a couples counselor is no different. They are trained to help your relationship succeed.

What can you expect from couples counseling?

A couples counselor can't save your marriage. That's up to you two. They can observe you, give you suggestions and homework, but it's up to you to follow through. Some important things to remember:

Be open. You must be willing to really look at yourself. Something has to change for this relationship to work and there's a good chance it needs to be you. It's easy to list all the things we can't stand about our partner, but it's a lot harder to hear what we're doing that pisses her off. Listen with an open heart. Change the things you can.

Understand you can't change her. You're probably going to counseling because you think she has a problem. You've got to stop looking at it that way. It's your relationship that has the problem; it's not necessarily her, but instead the way you relate to each other. Once you take the issue off the person and put it on the relationship, you both can focus on what you really need.

Don't expect a quick fix. Many big relationship problems have been brewing since before the two of you got together. We learn unhealthy ways of relating from our families, from our past relationships, from the way we feel about ourselves. Lifelong issues don't go away after one or two sessions. You should expect to spend a few months in therapy.

Talk honestly. The biggest issue couples need help with is communication. That's where the therapist can come in handy. She can observe your patterns, offer feedback, and give you skills to work on improving. She'll provide the tools, but you'll have to pick them up and use them.

Couples counseling, if you're both committed to doing what it takes, can be the kiss of life to your tattered and torn relationship.

Lipstick: Well, Dip, looks like those years of being a counselor for queer youth have paid off once again. You've covered it all. Nice job.

No Biting or Hair Pulling

Fighting fair

Lipstick: If there's one thing I hate more than fighting, it's when someone doesn't know how to play fair. Fighting is natural, healthy even to some degree, but if you're like Mike Tyson and you bite her ear off, it's not OK. You've got to learn how to fight fair. Here is a handful of things to consider when you're in the throes of battle:

Let a dead dog lie. And let the past stay where it belongs. Behind you. Don't continue browbeating her with mistakes she's made in the past. It will only cause resentment. Forgive and do your best to forget.

Play the game, but don't keep score. Are you a scorekeeper? Don't keep a running tally on the things you do and don't do in your relationship. Bringing up the fact that you did the grocery shopping three times in a row and the laundry four is not only tedious, but absurd. So is remembering that your partner broke plans with you two times the first year you were dating because of her softball games. Do you have nothing better to do with your time? Focus that energy instead on your relationship and let go of those silly numbers.

Never throw down the ultimatum card. Cack. I *hate* ultimatums. They're just glorified manipulations which typically end up blowing up in the user's face. At all costs, unless you're dealing with some sort of chemical dependency or adultery, do *not* ever give your partner an ultimatum.

Focus on the positive. Even when all you see is negative. When fighting, try to put a positive spin on your gripes. Don't say things just to get her riled up, or to intentionally hurt her feelings even if you're mad. I know it's tempting sometimes, but resist the urge. Try to make what you've got to say (or scream) as nice as possible. Remember, you love her and should *never* try to purposefully hurt her. If you take the low road, it will leave both of you feeling horrible and shallow.

Take it like a woman. Ouch. That criticism hurt. But she meant it so sincerely and not in a vindictive way at all. Don't you hate that? Me, too, but maybe we should listen. When your partner nails you to the wall about something you know you need to work on, it's best to take it to heart.

Deflect that deflection. Blame, blame, blame. Many dykes I know are really good at pointing their fingers. (If you're not careful, next time Lipstick sees you do this, she's going to break it off). It's time to take responsibility, girls.

Dump your defenses. What's wrong with being defensive?! Try to come from a place of calm and peace when fighting. I know it's an oxymoron and nearly impossible when she's yelling at you, but let her speak her mind. Don't be so quick to shut her down or interrupt. There are two of you in the relationship and both need to be heard, even if you think she's insane and her complaints baseless.

Believe it or not, she's flesh and blood. What a concept! To think that your girlfriend is actually human and allowed to not fit into the mold you've created for her is crazy, I know. You didn't see it in the first year you were together—thank you cunnilingus crack—but the fact is, she is, just like you, 75 percent water and as imperfect as the other seven billion people on this planet.

Refocus your lens. There's no better way to feel like shit than focusing on and pointing out your partner's flaws over and again. Telling her she's the most insecure person you've ever met and that it turns you off isn't going to do either of you any good. It won't make her more self-confident and it will make you feel like a heartless fool. Even when fighting, see her for the beautiful person she is.

Don't take her milk money. Don't bully and never make her feel like you're unapproachable. Eggshells suck. So does intimidation. She should be able to come to you about anything. I mean anything. Don't be someone who has such a thick skin that people are afraid of you.

See rainbows—not just green. Jealousy fucking sucks. If you're a jealous person, you'd best work on being more secure because it totally stems from your own shit. Granted, your girlfriend bumping and grinding with someone else on the dance floor —especially if she's smokin' hot—can make just about anyone jealous, but the origin of jealousy is still the same. It grows from you. Don't be jealous and, even if you are, be someone who recognizes it and works through it. (See section Broken Beer Bottles.)

DIPSTICK: Wow, Lip. You impressed me here. Perhaps this should be the topic of our next book.

Attention Friends: It's Her Side or Mine

Whom to talk to

You and your lover just had it out. It's the biggest fight you've ever had and it was a doozy. You finally decided to confront her about her not taking out the garbage and the next thing you know, she's laying out everything about your relationship that's bothering her. She says you never walk the dog, spend too much time with your mother, and always leave your lunch sack in the car. She is so angry she grabs her coat and screeches off down the street in your Volvo station wagon.

You're left stunned and wondering: Where did that come from? Obviously this is not about the dog, your mother, or your lunch sack. A million thoughts are going through your mind and you have to talk to someone. But who do you call? Are you being disloyal if you go to a mutual friend?

Lipstick: This is tricky business. If it were me, I wouldn't go to any of our mutual friends just yet. I'm not the type to air dirty laundry or maybe I'm too proud. I'd probably go for a run, and if I didn't have clarity after that, I'd journal for a while until I did. And if that didn't do it—which has only happened once—I'd call my brother the Swami. He and I were carved from the same stone and can usually finish each other's sentences, so I'd vent to him. He always gives good advice, I trust him wholeheartedly, and I don't mind being totally vulnerable at his feet.

Just because I have Swami doesn't mean your go-to guy or girl needs to be family. Find someone you trust, someone who isn't in love with you, someone who will be totally honest. And most importantly, someone who's going to take your side.

Going to the ex-girlfriend

She can be your best bet, or your worst. There are so many factors which play into this complicated choice; I'll do what I can to lay it out for you. There are five different kinds of ex-girlfriends, some you should call and some you shouldn't:

Don't call: the one who wants you dead. Obviously, you won't want to call the sketch ball you have a restraining order against. This might encourage her to go off her meds.

Don't call: the one who wants you back. Bad idea, and you know it. No matter how much you miss her and think she's just the person to help you work through this, she's not. You'll only give her false hope that your current relationship is over. She can't possibly give you impartial advice because all she can think about is how much she misses you and the dog.

Don't call: the one who couldn't give a shit. Don't be pathetic and call someone you know doesn't want to hear from you, no matter how much you still value her.

Do call: the one who wants the best for you. If you're lucky, your ex-girlfriend is one of your best friends. You've shared that most intimate part of yourself and she knows you better than anyone else—maybe even better than your current girlfriend knows you, depending on how long you were together. If you've somehow managed to come full circle and become great friends with no strings attached, count yourself lucky and count yourself among scores of other fortunate dykes. This ex can give you perspective, but don't go to her if you're not ready to hear the hard stuff. There were good reasons you broke up, after all. The problems in your current relationship aren't all about your girlfriend.

DIPSTICK: What if you don't keep in touch with any of your exes, Lip?

Lipstick: Show me a dyke who doesn't keep in touch with one of her exes and I'll show you a polar bear taking a dump in my tulip bed.

DIPSTICK: You'd better call *National Geographic,* because I haven't spoken to any of my exes in more than five years. And I certainly wouldn't dig their phone numbers up to process my current relationship. With a little tact, it is certainly fine to speak to friends about the big spat you and your girl had. We all need support from time to time.

If you have a best friend, she is a good one to call. She's always going to have loyalty to you and she's especially good when you just need validation that you're right and your girlfriend is dead wrong.

Any friend you had before you two got together is also fair game. He or she knows you pretty well, and has probably seen you in a few relationships. Listen to them.

You can also call your mother. Mamma just might lay it to you straight, let you know where you're playing into the dynamic, and tell you how she handles things with Dad when he storms off in their Cutlass Supreme.

Don't call someone you know will talk to other people and spread your dirt around town like a farmer on meth.

Lipstick: What?

DIPSTICK: Don't call her ex either to find out if she did this with her. That's just tacky. Do not call her best friend or anyone that the two of you consider to be both your friends. Call us. Or rather, send us an e-mail: ask@lipstickdipstick.com.

PART IV

Taking It to the Next Level

CHAPTER TEN

Here Comes the Bride

Y ou're certain she's the one. She's a true keeper and you can't imagine life without her. You want to spend the rest of your life with her and have twelve children. You want to shout your love from the tallest softball mound, or at least take out an ad in the local gay paper. And the best news is, she feels the same way! How did you get so lucky?

One great way to express your undying love and commitment to each other is to have a wedding, commitment ceremony, or Wiccan handfasting. While certainly not all couples need to express their love in this public manner, having your friends and family stand witness to your wedding vows is a very powerful experience.

Many report feeling different after their wedding—more committed, more legitimate—even if the law doesn't recognize it in most places. Before you say "I do" follow Lipstick & Dipstick's dos and don'ts.

She Got Down on Her Knees!

How to pop the question

DIPSTICK: My friend Lucia had been with her girlfriend Sal for three years. They were in love and Lucia wanted to pop the question. It had to be special and nontraditional, so she was racking her brain, trying to come up with a unique and meaningful way to do it.

Before Lucia could work out her plan, Sal surprised her by hiding an engagement ring in a bite of sushi. Lucia bit down into the Salmon

Dipstick's Quiz: How to Know It's Time to Take the Plunge

1. What do your friends think of your relationship:
   a. I haven't introduced her to my friends yet.
   b. they told me not to trust her, but I can't help it, it's love.
   c. our friends think of us as an old married couple.
2. What do you think about having children:
   a. she wants eight, but I don't like kids.
   b. we're not sure, but we're talking about it.
   c. we both want two—I'll have the first and she'll have the second.
3. Our relationship:
   a. is fire and ice, but when it's fire, it's *hot*.
   b. our sun signs are compatible, but our rising signs are not.
   c. I feel complete when I'm with her.
4. Before I get married I want to:
   a. sleep with as many women as possible.
   b. take my ad off *Curve* personals.
   c. make her a very special wedding gift.
5. The main reason I want to marry her is:
   a. so she doesn't go back to her ex.
   b. she asked and it's rude to say no.
   c. we have so much fun together.

Surprise roll and nearly broke her tooth. As she gingerly pulled it from her mouth, Sal got down on her knees and asked, *"Casamonos?"* (Will you marry me?) to which Lucia replied, "What?! What?! *Eres una loquita!"* (You're crazy.)

Here are some tips for the perfect proposal:

- Set a romantic tone. If you're going to ask her at home, have the place spit-shined, light candles, make her a nice dinner with sensuous foods.
- If you're going to ask her in a restaurant, make sure it's gay friendly.
- Valentine's Day is a great day to propose, but your anniversary and her birthday are also good choices.

6. How do you know she's the one:

    a. this is my third marriage and the third time is the charm.

    b. we both think the Pussy Cat Dolls are the best band that ever was.

    c. even our mothers get along.

7. Why get married if it's not legal:

    a. I need a new blender.

    b. I don't want to spend the rest of my life alone.

    c. we want all the people in our life to come together and publicly celebrate our relationship.

Tally, ho.

a = 0 points

b = 1 point

c = 2 points

10–14 Points: Call a florist and order that double bride cake topper. You two are a match made in heaven.

6–9 Points: I'm not saying you won't make it, but give it another year before you print the invitations.

5 or Fewer Points: Sorry kids, you're great fuck buddies, but no wedding bells for you.

Lipstick: I say all three of Dip's ideas are out. Make it a big surprise and pop the question when she's least expecting anything from you. Do something extraordinary!

DIPSTICK: Hold on, I've got a few more:

- Keep your sense of humor. If you get too serious, she'll start to freak out and think something is wrong.

- Include something from your first date. Propose to her at the coffee shop where you first met, play a song you liked to dance to, or prepare the same meal you served her that first night.

- Bring your personalities into it. If you're the hiking type, ask her atop a glorious mountain. If you're more the romantic type, have champagne and flowers while a jazz musician plays.

Ways NOT to propose:

- Through the announcer at a WNBA game.
- In bed.
- While driving.
- While making up from a big fight.
- On a billboard she drives past on her way to work.

Lipstick: I'll add:

- Less than a year after you've gotten together.
- At someone else's wedding.
- In front of her homophobic family.
- When she has the stomach flu.
- 24 hours after she's broken up with her girlfriend.

DIPSTICK: Who asks who? It doesn't really matter, as long as both of you want to spend your lives together.

I Always Dreamed of Wearing a Tuxedo

Planning the big day

Lipstick: A lot goes into planning a wedding. So much, in fact, that if you're having a full-blown, no holds barred event, then hiring a wedding coordinator is money well spent. Find a fagulous helper in the gay yellow pages and do it right, sister. What a wedding coordinator typically won't help you with is what you're going to wear—unless he's a friend, and especially if he's a queen, he might even have something you can borrow.

DIPSTICK: Don't dress to impress your faggy best friends. I say wear whatever you want. It's your wedding. Don't dress for your girl's grandparents. Do dress for each other and do make sure your outfits complement the other. Wear a tux and a long white gown. Wear the silk vests your friend Carol dyed by hand. Wear Birkenstocks and Bermuda shorts. Wear riding chaps and cowboy hats. When I got married, I was in my favorite black T-shirt and 501s.

Lipstick: Of course you were.

DIPSTICK: We were waiting in line outside San Francisco City Hall for hours. I had to be comfortable. Here are some things to ask yourself when planning your wedding.

Where are you getting married? On a windswept beach in Maui? Matching Hawaiian shirts are fine (as long as you never wear them at the same time again—barring your tenth wedding anniversary).

Lipstick: It's never OK to wear matching Hawaiian shirts. Did you hear me, girls? Never.

DIPSTICK: Whatever.

In a church or place of worship? Dress more conservatively. A tuxedo and dress are a good choice here.

Is it a formal wedding at your mom's country club? Then golf shoes and polo shirts are appropriate.

Lipstick: To me, that suggestion is like fingernails going across a chalkboard. It is OK to wear golf shoes and oxfords when you're golfing, but *not* when you're getting married, even if it is a hundred feet from a putting green. Getting married at a private country club? Fat chance if you're a gay couple. Getting married in a public country club? Wear something sexy and fashionable.

DIPSTICK: This age-old question comes up again and again: Should the butches wear tuxedos?

Pros of a tux

- You can rent it.
- It doesn't have to be cleaned.
- If you own it, you can have it tailored.
- Tails or no tails—your choice.

Cons of a tux

- Some women don't fit into a man's suit.
- Buying one is expensive and when are you going to wear it again? (Will Cris Williamson really play Carnegie Hall again?)

No matter what your tux choice, be sure you try it on and get it fitted properly.

Lipstick: Other things you should consider when planning a wedding:

Is there a chance it could rain and ruin your hair? If you're getting married in the Pacific Northwest, during monsoon season in Arizona, or somewhere else with temperamental weather, you must have a backup plan when it comes to an outdoor wedding. You'd hate to have to burn your wedding photos because your updo looked like a wet mop.

Will the wine pair well with dinner? Serving salmon for the main course? Then don't you dare serve merlot. And no white zinfandel either. In fact, don't serve white zinfandel ever again with anything. (It's fruit punch with a splash of moonshine.) If you must have white wine, pour a nice bottle of pinot rosé.

If you're serving roasted duck, how about a full-bodied red from Bordeaux? You won't be sorry. Be sure to consider these things when firming up the details of your wedding.

What color should your toenails be? I vote for French manicure on wedding days. It perfectly complements the purity of your love, and it goes with everything.

What kind of entertainment will you have? Will it be a jazz trio or your dyke friend who's a DJ? If you let Tammy Turntable do it, be careful about which songs hit the needle. Dykes go ape shit when they hear *My Neck, My Back* (you know the one: "All you ladies pop your pussy like this . . ."), but you'd best think twice before letting her spin that one. Granny might throw her hip out.

DIPSTICK: True story. The last time Dipstick wore a dress was in 1986 at my brother's wedding. I was a bridesmaid. (I'm sure those photos are going to surface one day on the Internet.)

Lipstick: They will if I have anything to do with it.

DIPSTICK: We had the fitting over Thanksgiving vacation. By the time the March wedding rolled around, Dipstick had put on a few pounds from mid-term exam stress. Not only was I in a dress which was not my color (fuchsia) or style (what dress is?), it was too tight. Could I have been any more uncomfortable? My advice to you brides and bridesmaids out there, lay off the Chunky Monkey between fitting and wedding date.

Be sure to bring your culture into the wedding. And by culture, I don't just mean ethnic culture. Bring your dyke culture in, too. Personally, I would love to be invited to a motorcycle wedding, with both brides in full riding gear, but feel free to wear a kilt, yarmulke, kente cloth, or oriental robe if those are part of your cultural heritage.

Or maybe you want to wear your mother's wedding gown? That would be special, unless you're a big butch like me. I wish I could have worn the suit my father got married in. Now *that* would have been hot! Vintage is in for weddings, but that can be expensive. Be sure to check out eBay for wedding dresses that were never worn. (Perhaps the bride came out as lesbian before the wedding!)

For the do-it-yourself dyke, why not make your wedding dress out of duct tape. What could be more lesbian than that?

Lipstick: I'll tell you what's more lesbian than that: wearing a dress dyed in rainbow colors, having your pet stand up as your best man, or a bride running off with the maid of honor.

Like Dipstick, I'm all for nontraditional, so I think *not* wearing a white gown is the thing to do. If it's what floats your boat, by all means, head to the bridal shop, but for you femmes out there, I think a nice spaghetti strap sexy kitten dress, in a shade which complements your complexion, is just what the dyke doctor ordered.

Dealing with parents

Dealing with parents, as well as antiquated traditions, can be sticky business. If your parents are cool enough to be a part of the big day, you don't want to burst their bubble, but at the same time, you don't want to do or have something you're not comfy with.

Lipstick:

When you're not sure they want to know. During the whole gay marriage boom in 2004, I knew a lot of dykes who got married without telling their parents.

Lipstick's Top Five Things Parents May Want You to Do Regarding Your Big Day

1. Register.
2. Not have sex until you're married.
3. Dance solo to kick off the party.
4. Throw the bouquet or your wife's garter.
5. Have your dad walk you down the aisle.

This was shocking to me. "They wouldn't be happy for me," one said in line at the county.

"They'd think it was ridiculous—they worked on George W. Bush's reelection campaign!" another claimed.

I not only found this sad, but also irritating. Telling your parents you're marrying your longtime girlfriend because you love her and want to spend the rest of your life with her even though you don't think they want to hear it is the *frontline* against the fight for civil rights. Don't coward out and take the easy road. Tell everyone.

Our issues regarding family and parents run the gamut when it comes to weddings and commitment ceremonies. No matter what you're dealing with, remember these key things. The first, be brave. The second is to stand your ground. The third, no matter how strained your relationship may or may not be, tell them! Don't deprive them of the opportunity to be a part of something so special. You never know, they might surprise you.

Dipstick's Top Five Things You Should Never Agree to, No Matter Who's Asking

1. Marry a man.
2. Sing your favorite karaoke song during the ceremony.
3. Invite your ex to be maid of honor.
4. Sleep with the stripper at your bachelorette party.
5. Use Styrofoam plates.

CHAPTER ELEVEN

Keeping Love Alive

This is the section you're going to come back to in twenty years. You'll dig *Lipstick & Dipstick's Essential Guide to Lesbian Relationships* out of a dusty attic box and the pages will fall open to this "Keeping Love Alive" chapter. You'll pull out your reading glasses and scan the pages. Then you'll put the book down and with your arthritic hands, you'll Google Lipstick & Dipstick to see where we are now, so you can send us a thank-you card.

In your tired hand, you'll thank us for all the tips we gave you that made your relationship the envy of all your friends and neighbors. You'll describe to us the twenty wonderful years you and your partner spent together and how, just when you were about to break up, fifteen years ago, you came upon this book in a bookstore and took our advice to heart. From that moment on, everything changed for you both. You fell back in love with each other and never fell out. You had amazing sex every night of the week, except for those two weeks she was recovering from back surgery, and raised six wonderful children. And you owe it all to Lipstick & Dipstick, because we gave you the tools to make your relationship the best it could be.

The credit really goes to you, dear reader. For you followed our advice, every little sassy detail. You celebrated with date nights, you never forgot an anniversary, you took wonderful vacations, and you kept your passion for the other things in your life. Yes, you worked hard to keep your love alive and for this, we applaud you!

Do You Come Here Often?

Date nights

DIPSTICK: Date nights are my favorite. Sometimes Tiger and I get a nice bottle of wine, some cheese and crackers and grapes, and sit on the back patio. It's special "us" time. We talk about what's going on in our community, how we're doing toward creating the life of our dreams, or just catch up on our busy lives.

Making time for dates is important. Just the act of dressing up and going out for a great dinner tends to put you in a different state of mind.

Get out of the house. Go to a movie instead of watching a video at home. Go out to dinner instead of ordering in a pizza. Get out and see a band instead of staying in and listening to CDs. At a loss for what to do? Here are some fun date ideas:

Casablanca Night: Eat at a Moroccan restaurant and visit a piano bar.

The High School Date: Share an ice cream sundae and watch a football game.

The Out-of-Town Date: Take a drive to a nearby tourist attraction—apple farm, pumpkin patch, winery—sample the goods and hold hands on the drive home.

The Weekend Date: Get out of town! Rent a cottage by the beach, stay at a lesbian bed and breakfast, or spend a weekend in Vegas. There's nothing like a change of scenery to spice things up.

The Surprise Date: Don't tell her where you're taking her. Just tell her how to dress. Do something unusual, like get tickets to a sold-out concert or end up at a picnic in the park.

The Game Date: Hide clues around the house. Like a scavenger hunt, each clue leads to something more tantalizing. Get your friends or favorite waitress involved, hiding clues all over town.

The Old Standby: Nothing is wrong with the old classic dinner-and-a-movie date. Romantic comedies are always a good choice, or take her to a sexy lesbian flick and you just might get lucky when you get home.

Lipstick: I, too, love date nights. Here are a few of my favorites.

Pussy Convention Date: Lying in front of the fire with all the pussies in the house—even if you have four fat cats—is so much fun. Not only can you get a little nooky from your purring girlfriend, but you can also make the cats feel like they're a part of it . . . even though they're so not. They don't know that, though. Here kitty kitty!

DIPSTICK: This creeps me out. I'm so glad I'm not dating you.

Lipstick: The feeling is mutual.

Red Light District Date: Go to an adult shop and pick out a movie and a new toy. Don't be afraid to explore your sexuality a bit. Maybe your girl has always wanted a teddy? A butt plug?

Double Down Date: Nothing turns me on like hearing my little Texas rose yell, *"Blackjack!"* Find your nearest casino and gamble the night away. You can even rent a penthouse suite if you win big.

Lions and Tigers and Queers, Oh My: Head to your local zoo to check out the animals. It's so much fun to pet the goats and watch the lions behind that heavy-duty fence. PS: Don't stick your finger through the chain-link into the monkey exhibit. Learned this the hard way.

Eight Ball in the Corner Pocket Date: Texas and I love to play pool. We often go neck and neck, so it makes it extra interesting when it comes down to the playoff . . . which usually happens in the bedroom afterward.

Flame Thrower Date: Saki, baby. Take your honey out for a Japanese teppanyaki dinner. It's so fun to watch them cook your food right there on the table. A word of warning, however—don't wear rayon. It's wildly flammable. You know how they throw fire from plate to plate? Well, one of those little balls of fire landed in my lap once and caught my dress on fire! It didn't do any permanent damage, just ruined my dress.

DIPSTICK: Glad you didn't end up with a smoking hoochy!

Lipstick: Me, too. Good thing I groom. They would have had to call 911 and spray you down with a fire extinguisher!

Anniversary Date: Never forget the important dates of your relationship. First date. First kiss. First shag. Wedding.

Dipstick: One last tip. Surprise her by taking her to her favorite restaurant, the one you don't like, or the opera, even though it puts you to sleep. She'll appreciate it.

Dust Off the Candles

Use your imagination

Dipstick: Some people wonder how Tiger and I are able to keep passion flowing between us after fifteen years together. Sometimes I wonder myself. Am I just lucky? Or am I doing something right? I prefer to think it's the latter. Here are some of Dipstick's special tips for keeping romance alive.

Dyke romance by Dipstick

- Make a point to tell her you love her. Say it when you mean it, not when you're trying to manipulate her. "Honey I love you so much, will you give me a back rub?"
- Buy her flowers and little tokens to say you care. It doesn't have to cost much. Buy her a T-shirt when you go out of town, or pick up some of her favorite muffins for a Sunday morning treat.
- Take her on a date. So many long-term couples don't date. It is essential to make time to do nothing except catch up with each other and your relationship. Tiger and I have a lesbian-owned wine bar we like to go to. We sit in our special table by the window, have a glass of chardonnay, and talk about why our life is so great. Plus gossip about the people at the next table.
- Meet her at the door after a long day's work with dinner, candles, and a special dessert. Later massage her sore feet and run her a hot bath.
- Encourage her dreams! Does she dream of being the next Isaac Stern? Buy her violin lessons. Does she want to be on *Survivor*? Help make her an audition tape. Always wished she had taken an art class? Buy her paints and an easel. The happier she is with herself, the happier she'll be with you.
- Follow your own passions. She fell in love with you because you were that crazy girl who loved rock climbing and live music. Just because

she doesn't share your love of granite is no reason not to head out climbing with your friends and hit the all-girl Clash tribute band later. The more you keep up with your passions, the more interesting you'll be to each other.

- Find a common interest. OK, you can't always be out chasing your own dreams. You have to have some passion you pursue together. Whether it's salsa dancing or viewing indie films, make dates to go to things you both enjoy.
- Follow through on your promises. If you say you'll take her clothes shopping this weekend, do it! Even if the big game is on. Did you promise to put your clothes in the hamper, instead of the floor, not leave your hockey skates in the front hall, and to walk the dog before you go to work? Believe it or not, these things will have an impact on your romantic relationship.
- Give her space when she needs it. Take some for yourself when called on.
- Have a sense of humor. Nothing keeps a relationship going longer than being able to laugh at yourself and your life. If you can make her laugh, long-term success is guaranteed.

Lipstick: Dip, I gotta hand it to you and Tiger—fifteen years is quite a feat. Texas and I just passed the seven-year mark. I agree with everything on your dyke romance list and I'd like to add a couple things. The first is always tell her how nice she looks. Even if you hate the pants she's wearing or think her hair looked better long. Let her believe she's the most beautiful woman in the world! And she is.

Second, be sure to always keep the seductress within on call.

Are you the femme fatale in your relationship? Or do you always let your girlfriend take the lead?

Texas and I are both seductresses, which is why our sex life is still alive. Wanna know the magic formula to be a killer siren? Zero inhibitions plus preparation plus imagination.

For those of you who didn't get it honestly, here are some tips:

Let yourself go. When it comes to the bedroom, you've got to completely let yourself go, ladies. Leave your inhibitions at the door and show your lover a good time.

Ready, set, prepare. Have a plan. Think about what you're going to do to her and get everything ready. We're talking lit candles, music streaming, cued video, plenty of lube, etcetera.

Imagination. Don't be a robot. Don't just get the job done in time to watch *Desperate Housewives.* Take your time and use that creative mind of yours. Role-play or try some new positions in the bedroom.

Speak up. Also in the sack, one of the best ways to get the party started is through what you say. Talk dirty. Talk sexy. Seduce her with words. Writer Marya Mannes once said: "All great lovers are articulate, and verbal seduction is the surest road to actual seduction." Bedroom talk is often hampered by inhibitions.

   If you find yourself afraid to speak up, check out this book from the library. It's geared toward heterosexual sex, but it's useful: *Electrify Your Sex Life: How to Get Rid of Sexual Hangups and Inhibitions and Open Yourself to Pure Pleasure* by Carole Altman, Ph.D.

DIPSTICK: We grow up hearing so many negative things about sex—especially as women—and doubly so as lesbians. It's a wonder we orgasm at all!

   Despite the best efforts of those Bible-banging pundits, somehow we keep coming out of the closet, keep falling in love, and keep having fantastical sex. As women, we were born to have sex. The female body is a sexual capsule. The clitoris is there for one thing only: our enjoyment. Wouldn't it be a shame to not let this little piece of anatomy do its job?

   Even though we're born sexual beings, we're not born natural lovers. That, my friend, takes learning and practice. And like most things in life, it's those who seek lifelong knowledge who are most satisfied. Make a commitment to keep learning and growing your sexual repertoire.

Some books you might want to consider adding to your library:

The Whole Lesbian Sex Book: A Passionate Guide for All of Us by Felice Newman

On Our Backs Guide to Lesbian Sex by Diana Cage

Lesbian Sex by JoAnn Loulan

Ultimate Guide to Cunnilingus by Violet Blue

Tantric Sex for Women by Christa Schulte
The Ultimate Guide to Strap-On Sex by Fairy Butch

No matter where you go or what you read, remember that this is your sex life. You are in the driver's seat, so why not take the most scenic route possible. Don't just take the safe highway.

Meet Me in the Bedroom between Yoga and the Rally

Making time for sex

Lipstick: We're all busy, right? But do you feel like sometimes you're busier than anyone else you know? When you're hectic and you're in a long-term relationship, it's way too easy to put sex at the end of the to-do list. Especially if you have kids. In fact, I bet you're so busy that you're on the elliptical at the gym reading this book—multitasking, as usual.

A good sex life is subjective. I'm not going to tell you that you *must* have sex at least once a week to have a healthy sex life. Why? Because how often you have sex, and how comfortable you are with how much (or how little) is yours to gauge. I'm just here to tell you that you *must* not ignore sex and you must not ignore that you and your girlfriend are ignoring sex. Comprende?

Last summer, Texas and I were busy little bees. Our normally garden-centric weekends were filled with out-of-town guests, writing projects, and lots of trips. Even though we did make time to open the garden and get a layer of mulch down before the weeds started poking through, we didn't have any time for upkeep. Pruning and weeding kept getting pushed off until the next weekend; the grass needed mowing but the blades on the mower needed sharpening. There was always an excuse, life, and procrastination coming between us and the garden.

It wasn't until mid-summer that we slowed down and stepped outside to see how the garden looked. And wouldn't you know, low and behold, most of the garden had died. Those plants that hadn't shriveled up were choked with weeds and barely hanging on. Right there under our noses, all the beauty that once was had dried up.

"How did this happen?" I screamed.

"I don't know!" Texas echoed.

Hindsight tells me exactly how it happened. If you don't tend to the garden, those sweet little buds of life will die. The same applies to the intimacy of your relationship. If you don't continue to make it a priority, continue watering, trimming the deadheads, and tending to any diseases that sneak into your garden of love, you'll wake up one day too and realize you and your girlfriend are no longer lovers, but roommates.

So, standing in our backyard in horror, we had five options:

1. We could stand firm in our dismay and blame each other for not making time.
2. We could put down our lemonade, grab a hoe, and each take care of separate portions of the garden. (Lipstick note: be careful what kind of hoe you grab. The one without the "e" will only get you in trouble.)
3. We could put a shot of vodka in the lemonade, cuddle in the hammock, and try to laugh about it.
4. We could break up and sell the house.
5. We could work together to get the garden back in shape, understanding that resuscitating something so fragile takes diligence, patience, and time.

What did we do? Number three followed by number five.

DIPSTICK: Great analogy, Lipstick. I'm sure with some gentle coaxing, lubrication, and sweet talk, your garden was flourishing once more. To see your sex life blooming again, you don't have to schedule an all-day work party. Just check in a few times a week or month, as the case may be. Add a little fertilizer while the meat marinates. Instead of checking in with Katie Couric after work, tackle your honey on the couch and nibble her toes before you nibble on the corn.

Once you get in the habit, like going to the gym and eating breakfast, having regular sex will be just that—regular. As we grow comfortable with each other, our desire naturally wanes. Who could keep up if it stayed as intense as it was at the beginning of our relationship anyway?

If you're in a relationship and you aren't having sex, try this experiment. Pick a day of the week, whether it's Sunday morning or Friday after work. Nothing else can happen until at least one of you orgasms. If you're one of those people stressing out about too much on her plate, you're likely to orgasm first, so you can get out of bed and finish the tasks on your list. Ah, but hopefully what will happen is, once the tingling subsides, you'll realize that there really is nothing more important to do (or rather nobody more important) than staying in bed and ringing her bell.

Palm Springs or Provincetown?

Getting away together

Lipstick: If you're like me, you like to go on vacation. And if you're even more like me, you like to go away several times a year. And if even more, you like to have lots of other homos around while you're taking a load off.

For my partner and me, it sucks when we go on vacation and realize, once we've settled into our room, that we're the only gay people for a hundred miles. But that might not be the case for everyone out there. Whether you want to be surrounded by rainbow Speedos or sipping Peppermint Paddies in the ski lodge with a gaggle of fags, as moes, we have to be strategic when we plan our vacations. With all the good and bad choices, it can be complicated.

What compounds things even more: both of you are trying to decide on one place to spend your coveted time off. With one relationship come two different personalities. With two different personalities come two different sets of desires; not only for food and sex, and daily minutiae like groceries, movies, and social entertainment, but also for vacations. For your winter getaway, one of you wants to go fly-fishing in Chile, the other wants to hit the Christmas markets in Germany. When it's summertime, she wants to go to Provincetown and you want to get a good start on your tan in San Diego. So many destinations, so little time. Here is a breakdown of your choices that will make it easier to navigate.

Gay-centric vacay. Lesbos here we come! Do you love being surrounded by your dyke sisters? Well, then, there are lots of great choices for you and your honey in the summertime. Provincetown in the summer is the place to be, as is a bevy of other great places. Other gay-centric destinations

Lipstick recommends include West Hollywood, Key West, Cabo San Lucas, Mykonos, Palm Springs, Fort Lauderdale, and, of course, the Isle of Lesbos, Greece.

You mustn't forget the glorious Olivia Cruises, which will float you and hundreds of other dykes all over the world.

Beyond these queer destinations, there are many great gay weeks or gay weekends. These include Aspen's Gay and Lesbian Ski Week, Dinah Shore Weekend in Palm Springs, Gay Days in Orlando, Sydney Mardi Gras, and many more.

DIPSTICK: Lipstick, how can you forget our neighbor to the north? Some of my favorite vacations have been in the country of gay marriage: Vancouver, Toronto, and Montreal. All wonderful dyke-friendly destinations.

Lipstick: Totally, Dip. Oh Canada slipped my mind. Great ideas.

For additional information about traveling the queer way, check out Planetout.com/travel.

Gay-deficient vacay. Recently, Texas and I went on vacation to Maui. We had a lovely time . . . except, I'm convinced, we were the only homos on the Hawaiian island. Well, that's not entirely true. There were two men with waxed chests sipping mai tais near the waterfall who were questionable. And, while we were at Cheeseburger Paradise in Lahaina, a lesbian couple walked by—both with telling mullets and matching Hawaiian shirts (ladies, see Lipstick's Fashion Tips for Couples). With wide eyes, they looked at us like we looked at them: Oh my god! Lesbians!!

If you don't care about being around other gay people, feel free to book a trip to wherever your heart desires. Odds are you'll get what you want. Most popular destinations are swarming with heteros and their screaming kids. (Aren't screaming kids parented by gay folks so much less annoying?)

DIPSTICK: Don't forget the new LGBT family vacation R Family Cruises (rfamilyvacations.com) and family week in P-town. Better yet, send the kids off to Camp Ten Trees (camptentrees.org) and rent that yurt on the coast for a week.

Lipstick: Good suggestions.

The closeted vacay. There are lots of scary places out there, so even though it's not something we normally do, occasionally, depending on the circumstances, in foreign countries we must put our asses in the closet. What Téjas and I like to do is travel with a male gay couple; that way, you've got men around and, if need be, you can just latch arms with one of the dudes if you feel you're in danger. It's genius. They're like an "in case of emergency" husband.

DIPSTICK: While Maui and Barcelona with your "husbands" may be great choices for vacations, don't think you have to save for six years to get away. In fact, escaping at least four times a year is essential, to give yourself perspective, to take a break from life's stresses and rejuvenate your love life.

One of Dipstick's favorite vacations was when the Tiger Lady and I rented an RV and went camping in the Grand Canyon. We hiked and saw all kinds of wildlife: bald eagles, a cougar, coyote, and a California condor. We looked up each animal in a Native American spirituality book to see how it related to our lives.

Even if we can't afford to traipse across Europe, Tiger and I make sure to take overnights to the coast, spend a few days camping, or even go visit friends who live out of town.

One bed or two?

How many times has this happened to you? You pore through travel brochures and Web sites to find the perfect, romantic hotel. You get the corner room, with the king-size bed and the great view. Then when the two of you show up to check in, the front desk clerk starts to freak out, like they made a mistake getting you a room with only one bed. Here are three ways you can handle it:

1. No, no, it's OK. We're sisters and we grew up sharing the same bed.
2. How could you! We'll take the crappy room, but we demand a free night!
3. Sure, give us the room with two beds. We always dreamed of having one bed just for sex and the other for sleeping.

Lipstick: Another way to handle it would be to whip out your dildo and threaten them with it . . . that is *if* your dildo made it to your destination.

Sex toys are tough to travel with. You really just have two choices when it comes to traveling with vibrating accoutrement—checking them or carrying them on—both with enormous risks.

I have a nightmare story to share. Years ago, Texas and I were traveling to visit some fag friends in DC. At the time, we were living in different states and our relationship was brand spankin' new, so you know what that meant—*lots of frantic sex*. We'd been together long enough that we'd invested in quite a few sex toys. I carried them all to our destination and, needless to say, was glad I brought them along. We had our own place and each morning to do whatever our pussies desired.

After a great three-day weekend, we caught our flight, which was insanely late, and barely made our connection in Philadelphia. We're talking right-out-of-a-movie sprint to the gate. We made it safely home, but our luggage didn't. Hers eventually did, but mine was lost forever, six sex toys dissolved into the dark Philly vortex never to be seen again. Worse yet, the luggage tag on my suitcase had my *parent's* address on it. I had nightmares of it showing up, torn open with its contents in a clear plastic box—my father holding up the box, looking inside, and never seeing his little girl in the same light again. I also had nightmares of airport workers throwing Swirly around like it was a Nerf football, or the Purple Pussy Eater hanging humorously from the bulletin board.

Despite being permanently scarred (I hate US Airways), I still check those little fuckers because it continues to be the better option. Haven't you seen the poor people at security who are pulled aside for a rummage through their skid-marked underwear?

I do check 'em, but I'm much more thoughtful about which toys I bring along. I don't pack the whole satchel of nipple clamps anymore nor our best leather harness. And just like the President and the Vice-President can't fly on the same plane, neither can the Rabbit Habit and the Water Dancer.

DIPSTICK: What the hell is this Water Dancer you keep mentioning? I even Googled it and came up dry!

Purposeful Pedestal

Respecting each other

Lipstick: We must. We must. We must increase our bust! And respect our girlfriends!

If you don't respect your partner, forget about having any kind of relationship. You might as well fold now and cut your losses. Respect is a salient ingredient in any successful relationship—romantic or not.

When she's not the sharpest tool in the box

If you think your girlfriend is an idiot, you're headed for trouble. In order to make it, we must respect our girl and believe she's wickedly smart and funny. She's got to be surprising and charming and absolutely delightful . . . to you at least. Your friends don't have to hold her with the same esteem— that's a whole other issue—but you must think she hangs the moon.

DIPSTICK: Ain't that the truth! Humor and intelligence are subjective, but the two of you should be able to get each other's jokes and laugh together at all the other morons out there. But if you think your gal is also a moron, then pack it in right now.

Back when Dipstick was in her youth, she met a softball player named Marti. Marti was cute as hell, had a great ass, and a great sense of humor. Marti and I had a blast together, riding bikes, taking hikes, and going dancing two or three nights a week. I was in college at the time and into having all kinds of political and philosophical discussions with my friends. But Marti, having barely made it out of high school, couldn't really keep up with the intellectual feminist union crowd. And when she did occasionally pipe in with her opinion, someone from the crowd usually challenged her and she was left stammering and sucking on her beer bottle. It's not that Marti wasn't intelligent; she just didn't have access to the same information we college snobs did. Unfortunately, I was young and foolish and didn't realize that at the time, so I didn't respect her. Instead, I was ashamed when she'd tag along with my fiercely feminist friends. It wasn't her fault, but clearly we weren't meant to be together.

Lipstick: Poor Marti.

My bitch kicks ass

I think my wife is superfly, and you should, too. I respect her in so many ways, and as our relationship grows, that list only gets longer. She challenges me, she pushes me, she doesn't roll over for anyone, and she's never wrong. OK, well the fact that she's hardheaded isn't my favorite thing about her, but I do appreciate a woman who believes in herself. Besides, as we've aged, she's had to fight even harder for this position, because we both have learned that I'm the one who usually ends up being right. About 80 percent of the time. The girl stands up for herself and what she believes in and I think that's not only respectable, but also very sexy.

Dipstick: Oh yeah, well . . .

My bitch can kick your bitch's ass

Well, Tiger is superfunny and smart as hell. And you should see her in her running outfit. She's willing to talk about the hard stuff, but doesn't dwell on it, well at least when I tell her to stop dwelling on it. She makes a great home for our family and sometimes I feel she's the only one who really gets me. So, I make sure to tell her everyday that I love her and that she's cute, or hot or sexy or whatever she is at that moment. I make sure I mean it when I say it, because if there's one thing Dipstick can't do, it's lie, remember?

Lipstick: We remember, Dip. Beyond saying sweet things, it's important to understand that respect is different than love. Love is a profoundly tender affection for another person. Love is the fuzzy stuff. The playful names you call her. The little notes you stick in her lunch. The passionate way you look into her eyes when you make love, or even when just fucking in the backseat. Respect is something else. Respect is esteem for your girl, or the sense of the worth you place on her as a human, as a woman. Your respect for her may be rooted in one of her qualities or abilities, or perhaps it's a manifestation of all she does. The way she moves through the world.

DIPSTICK: So that even when she does something really stupid, something that you'd never do, you don't put her down, or say "I told you so." Respect is about acknowledging her feelings, even when you don't agree with them. Respect is about standing up for her, no matter what. Respect is about walking away for some breathing room when you're too angry to talk. Respect is about treating her the way you want to be treated. Respect is hard to define, but it is key to a healthy relationship.

Lipstick: You're right, Dip. It is key.

Show yourself some props

Equally as important as respecting your partner is respecting yourself. Nothing is more of a turnoff than a woman who thinks she sucks. We hear from so many women who don't respect themselves. They don't even try to hide it most times. They'll flat out admit it. Why would you stick around in an abusive relationship? Why would you keep taking her back even though she's cheated on your four times? It's because you don't respect yourself—you'd never treat someone you respect the way you treat yourself. If you're lacking in this area, friends, it's time to do some work. Browse the self-help section at your local bookstore. There are tons of books out there.

DIPSTICK: Here, here, Lipstick. Self-esteem is not something you just wake up with one day. Like coming out, it's a lifelong process. It can go up and it can go down. Sometimes we might feel all great about ourselves, confident that we're the best poet this side of Omaha or one hot Latin dancer and then the smallest thing will knock us down. We trip during the open dance competition or our play gets a bad review.

We get beat down, we build back up again. Having a stable and loving partner can help through those low esteem times, like when you fail a class or you pronounce the boss's name wrong in front of the whole company. Those are the times you need someone to remind you how talented, or smart, or funny, or brilliant you are. You need someone who has saved every poem you've ever written and who has your paintings framed and hanging in the den (besides your mother). You need someone who will tell you that it's OK to make mistakes and that that's how we learn and grow and someone who will remind you how far you've come. So, no, you can't be in a relationship if you don't respect yourself or your girlfriend, but a good love can help you through those times when your esteem is battered.

It's More Than a Painted-On Smile

Passion to live life to the fullest

Lipstick: I drive Dipstick crazy with my passion for life.

DIPSTICK: It's true. Every week she's handing me a new self-help tape to listen to or giving me some kind of fertility god to put on my desk. I've just set up a little corner of my office I like to call Lipstick's Latest Craze.

Lipstick: In addition to the shrine Dip's had to create, it may be that on most mornings I spring inspired from bed before sunrise, or that occasionally I squeal when I write something witty. It may be that I like to push Dipstick out of her comfort zone and cram motivational tapes or the latest self-help book down her throat. Whatever it is, I just can't help myself.

However, I don't live in a vacuum, so I understand what works for me, doesn't work for everyone else.

DIPSTICK: Yes, that 6:00 A.M. heart meditation didn't really do it for me.

Lipstick: Yeah, I know. You were snoring.

If you're like me or not, there are few universal things that I'd like to get across:

The time is now. We must, absolutely MUST live life right now, and live it hard! There's no guarantee you or your relationship will be around tomorrow.

DIPSTICK: I believe that. Why just this evening, Tiger came down to my office to chat before her hair appointment. I was deep in work and didn't stop what I was doing to properly send her off and wish her a wonderful haircut. Next thing I knew, three hours had gone by and she wasn't home yet. I didn't really start to panic, but the weather outside was nasty and I began to worry something had happened to her. Finally she showed up, with her hair all shiny and new. Turns out, she was not only getting a cut, but a dye job.

My point is this, as I fretted she might never return home, the thoughts in my head were *Was that going to be the last interaction we ever had? When I ignored her and didn't take five minutes from my work to say I love her?* Yes, the time is now. Don't put off for tomorrow what you can do today!

Lipstick:

No excuses! Famed entrepreneur Don Wilder once said, Excuses are the nails used to build a house of failure.

And Lipstick couldn't agree more. If there are two things I am repulsed by it is apathy and excuses. I hate them equally and so will the woman you're dating.

Beyond getting rid of excuses, be proactive about your life. If you or your partner is miserable in your current job or your physical health, then do something about it! If you say you don't have time to pursue your passion, then get up earlier and take small steps to get there. Don't just sit around and let your lives slip away or steep in unnecessary toxins.

I am intention and you should be, too

Even if new age positive thinking isn't for you and you wouldn't dare put a Ganesha on your desk (especially if you don't know who Ganesha is), one thing you must understand is that you'll never get anywhere without intention.

Do you want your relationship to be more affectionate?

Do you want to buy that house on the river?

Do you want to open that coffee shop together like you talked about when you first started dating?

Do you want to have a million dollars in the bank by the time you're fifty?

If so, the power lies inside you to make these dreams come true. You've just got to learn how to harness that universal energy in the right way. Lipstick believes that everything in this world is connected and that we manifest what we intend into our lives. You use this power everyday, even though you don't realize it.

Do you want you and your girlfriend to talk more honestly? Do you wish to stop feeling so jealous each time another woman looks at her? Then let those things be your intention and work hard to get there.

Intrigued? Check out Wayne Dyer's *Power of Intention*.

Another little gem that will help you reach goals: *Success Principles* by Jack Canfield.

DIPSTICK: Sorry folks, sometimes I just have to let Lipstick go. It's easier than trying to get a muzzle on her.

Dynamic Duos

Spending time with other couples

Lipstick: I love eating out—it's my favorite thing to do. I also enjoy going out to dinner, both on romantic dates with my honey and with good friends. There's nothing like kickin' it with other couples, whether you're out to happy hour, going to the theater, or breaking bread at a restaurant or in someone's backyard, it's healthy (or it should be) to spend time with other couples. When it comes to those couples we hang with, they come in all shapes and forms. Here are a few:

The Time Bomb: a.k.a. Ellen and Anne. This is the couple who seems fine on the outside—they don't have public fights and things appear hunky-dory, even though you have one eyebrow up because a subtle nag inside tells you something ain't right. You pass it off and continue spending time with them until one day you wake up and *wham*, one of them is on the news, lost in some suburban neighborhood, ringing doorbells and speaking in some madcap terrestrial language. "The mother ship is coming," she says to the camera and you stare in disbelief, understanding at that moment that your intuition is always right.

   This couple can also be flagrant about their explosive ways. Always fighting, nitpicking, and nagging each other. Be careful about spending too much time with a Time Bomb, ladies. Volatile energy is no good for your relationship. Limit your exposure because you might get hurt when they finally blow.

The Rock: a.k.a. Melissa and Tammy. How refreshing. You love spending time with this couple because they're fun and they're so damn easy to be with. You want to do everything with them because they're not only a blast, but because being around another healthy couple who believes in open communication and proactive maintenance—as opposed to passive aggressive behavior and conniving—is good for your relationship, too.

Brangelina: a.k.a. Brad and Angelina. Straight, but not narrow. The cool heterosexual couple. So, you might have a crush on the female, but what's the harm? You've given the husband an honorary dyke medal, sure he was a lesbian in his former life, and the wife appreciates a little girl on girl, even if she's never had her some. Or maybe she has. You have much in common with this couple, politics included. Sure you may fight different ground battles on Election Day—they're concerned about public schools funding; you, making sure they don't throw you in jail for being gay—but beyond that, you fight the good fights together. You love the same restaurants. You love the same theater. You love to play Trivial Pursuit on a rainy night in front of the fire. You all have been dying to go scuba diving in Belize. You heart these straight people and they heart you.

DIPSTICK: I'll add a few more, Lip.

The Neighbors: a.k.a. Monica and Chandler. These are the people you spend the most time with, mainly because they live next door and you're always there borrowing a tent or asking them to watch your cat while you're away. Oftentimes with The Neighbors, you end up drinking bottles of wine until late in the night and learn more about each other's sex lives than you care to remember the next morning. These are the people who are there for you when the power goes out, when you need a cup of sugar, or your car is broken into.

The Colleagues: a.k.a. Cagney and Lacey. You work with lots of people, but these are the folks you really like. Your boss may have you over for dinner, or you may go out drinking with the only other queers on staff. Work friendships are important. Not only can they make life on the job more fun, but they may also be essential when it's time for that promotion.

Lipstick: Yes, Dip, you're right! We could go on forever describing the many wonderful couples, and those that are not so wonderful, in our lives, but this is the bottom line: Positive sustenance in, positive substance out. Garbage in, garbage out. We are only as good as those we spend time with, so choose your friends wisely and guard them with your life.

DIPSTICK: Friendships are very important. Why, it was my friend Rex who grabbed me by the shoulders and shook me once when I was about to cheat. "I know you and Tiger are having problems," she said. "But this is only going to make things worse." She was right. Thank Goddess she stopped me. I don't think I can ever repay Rex for that.

Then there was my friend Lori who I trained for the triathlon with. My friend Dawn who I would go to punk rock shows with, and my friend Lipstick who helped me get one of my first writing jobs. Friends help pick you up when things are bad. Friends are there to celebrate life's successes with. I also know how vital they are when you're going through a rough time. When someone in my group of friends was dying of cancer, we all rallied, not only to support her, but to support one another.

Our partners can't be the world to us. After the cunnilingus crack wears off, be sure to get back in touch with the important friends in your life and hold them near like a pair of puppies in your lap.

Start That Roller Derby League

Keeping your own interests

Kelly and Wanda had been together for four years. Before they met, Kelly played the cello and loved listening to live jazz. Wanda was on a queer water polo team and used to lifeguard on the weekend at the beach. As with most couples, when they fell in love, they shut themselves out from the world (remember the dyke gestation period?). This is all fine and good . . . for awhile. The problem with Kelly and Wanda was that they never opened back up.

Lipstick: Have you cut yourselves off from the world? Are there things you used to do "before relationship" (B.R.)? Do you find yourself dreaming about hitting a hockey puck and kicking ass on the ice like you did way back in 2003 B.R.? Remember how you liked to take cooking lessons in 2004 B.R.? Contrary to popular dyke perception, it's actually OK to do things without your beloved; in fact, it's healthy.

Here is a list of things Texas likes to do without me. Perhaps this will spark some ideas for you in case you don't do a damn thing alone:

- Antique shop
- Low-impact aerobics
- Paint
- Watch black-and-white movies
- Lie in front of the fire with the cat
- Collect various tchotchkes
- Collect Daphne du Maurier books
- Watch Lifetime movies
- Scrub the kitchen floor
- Read under the heating blanket
- Roller skate
- Do laundry
- Garden

Here's a list of what Lipstick likes to do without her princess:

- Run
- Take long baths
- Write
- Rake leaves
- Light candles
- Go shopping
- Ride my bike
- Eat sushi
- Browse the shelves at Powell's bookstore
- Rollerblade
- Get buried in a coffee shop with my laptop on a rainy day
- Karaoke
- Snowboard
- Meet Dipstick for coffee and talk about all of you

Alone time

Texas and I love spending time together, but we also love our alone time. I've seen many couples denounce alone time, saying they just can't stand being apart. Is that you? If so, I encourage you to buck the system and let go of her hand for just a little while. Start small. You go to one side of the living room and have her go to the other. Now sit there for an hour. Next, try different rooms. After that, we're ready for one of you to leave the house. Remember to take a cell phone in case you have separation anxiety.

DIPSTICK: Dipstick loves to see live concerts. Tiger would rather stay at home and listen to the CD, but not too loud. Dipstick loves to check out new restaurants. Tiger would rather stick to the tried and true favorites. Dipstick takes long bike rides to clear her head. Tiger goes running with the dog.

Spending time alone is not only important, it's necessary; so is taking the time to do the things you cherish, that your partner doesn't care that much about. Sometimes you can drag her along and she'll be a good sport, but if there's something you love, that your new love doesn't, don't despair. Instead, keep doing it—alone or with your buddies.

Look at straight people. For eons the men have gone off hunting while the wives hold quilting bees and bake sales. Even new age hippie straights split up. My brother takes Cuban drum lessons while his wife is on a shamanic journey to Peru. Going away for a weekend is a great thing because it usually means great "welcome home" sex.

No matter how long you've been together—a week or over a decade—always remember to keep a good balance in your life.

Imagine Your Future

Dreaming together

"To accomplish great things, we must not only act, but also dream; not only plan, but also believe."

—ANATOLE FRANCE

DIPSTICK: It's important to have goals and dreams, both as individuals and as a couple.

Lipstick: I agree. Texas and I keep a journal of our dreams/goals, which we dig into twice a year. We started this tradition when we first got together.

In the beginning, our goal-setting manifested on dive bar cocktail napkins where we'd hunkered down for happy hour. We've since graduated to a classy suede journal and a bottle of Veuve Clicquot, but the sentiment is the same. We set goals each year and work hard to reach them.

We love keeping this journal because it's amazing to go back and see what we've accomplished. In this crazy world, it's easy to forget how far you've come both in your career and in your relationship. It's critical to reflect and celebrate the victories, the stars you've pulled from the sky.

Five things from our first list:

1. Buy a house
2. Have sex five days a week
3. Lipstick to get her own column
4. Texas to get her real estate license
5. Go to Hawaii for first time

Five things from our most recent list:

1. Remodel house
2. Have sex twice a week
3. Lipstick to get her own reality show with Dipstick
4. Texas to sell seventy-five houses this year and be the top seller in her office
5. Buy a vacation house on Maui

See how far we've come? This goal-setting business works!

DIPSTICK: Hey, Lip, those are great goals, but don't forget that you can also create the kind of relationship you want by setting goals. When dreaming about the future, it helps to be specific—and why not write them as affirmations?

For the single gal: I'm in a loving committed relationship with a girl who totally gets me.
For the bickering couple: We have open and honest communication, listening and supporting each other.
For the lesbian bed death: We have a wonderful, passion-filled relationship.

Lipstick: Good examples, Dip.

Obviously, it takes more than affirmations to make a relationship work—that's why we wrote this book—but it certainly helps.

Together, with one unified voice, Dipstick and I would like you to understand the power that lies within all of us to create the life we want. Believe in the future and believe in who you are—both separate and together. Never dwell on the past and always remember: The couple who dreams together stays together.

EPILOGUE

Dear readers,

So, here we are . . . at the end.

We enjoyed our journey with you and hope you did, too. We also hope you were able to glean a tidbit or twenty that you'll apply to your own life and partnership. With nearly thirty years of relationship experience, in our butch and femme glory, we must be doing something right.

Maybe Texas and Tiger will write a response to this book and include things we may've left out, like how important it is to forgive, or what to do when you've both got hellacious cramps and there's only one Advil left.

As we look back through the chapters, it seems there are really two key ingredients in a successful partnership:

Good communication and sex.

Both of which you must have to survive the long haul. You probably knew this before you picked us up, but here's the confirmation. You don't have to be having sex every day (and certainly not right this minute at the library or bookstore) or have a heart-to-heart each morning before you make the coffee, it just means you need to be constantly aware and always strive for the best of both.

Until next time, be horny, be faithful, and be well.

Yours truly,
Lipstick & Dipstick

PS: Don't put this book down just yet—turn the page and check out the Gay Girl's Glossary.

We'd love to hear from you: ask@lipstickdipstick.com

LIPSTICK & DIPSTICK'S
GAY GIRL'S GLOSSARY

Carpet picnic: A romantic dinner eaten on the living room floor (preferably in front of a fire or surrounded by candles).

Cunnilingus crack: The cause of the sex-crazed narcosis we're thrown into when we fall in love.

Dental dam: Silly flap of latex that got its start in dentists' offices, but made its claim to fame spread across the beautiful beaver (a.k.a. cum curtain, sexy shade, hoo hoo hoody, labia lingerie).

Dry as a bone syndrome: A serious disorder that means your pussy can't produce juice (a.k.a. female sexual arousal disorder).

Dyke gestation period (DGP): The superimportant six months in the beginning of your relationship when you simply date, live in separate places, and enjoy falling in love.

Gaydar: That sense you get when you know someone's gay, whether they know it or not.

Gold star: A dyke who's never slept with a man.

Hand me the remote syndrome (HMRS): A serious disorder that means no sex drive for you (a.k.a. inhibited sexual desire).

Heart fuck: When you're having an affair with a certain someone who you haven't actually touched (a.k.a. emotional cheating).

Heavy immersion: During the Preliminary Pussy Period, it is tryouts on steroids.

Homo no-no: Something that gay people should never do.

Human papillomavirus (HPV): A sexually transmitted disease caused by human papillomavirus, which is a group of viruses that includes more than one hundred different strains or types. It can lead to cervical cancer.

Kegelism: A serious disorder with a funny name that means you have a hard time letting anything into your pussy (a.k.a. vaginismus).

Long-term relationship (LTR): Duh.

Make-out vacation: This is a vacation for women whose partners travel for work and take advantage of the out-of-town rule (see below). On this vacation, you get to make out with as many women as you'd like with no strings attached.

Masturbation mania: When you're masturbating so much you don't want to have sex with your partner anymore.

Mind the vagine: The state of mind where you're not frightened by what turns you on.

Mo: HoMOsexual.

Nobody's home disorder: A serious disorder that means no orgasm for you (a.k.a. anorgasmia).

Only-child syndrome: When you're raised an only child and have a hard time sharing.

Out-of-town rule: When you're out of town, you get to make out with other chicks.

Penis envy: When you really wish you had a penis.

Polyamory: Participation in multiple and simultaneous loving or sexual relationships.

Poontang: Your pussy (a.k.a. poon, the girl, hoo hoo, ya ya, chocha, yum yum).

Preliminary Pussy Period (Triple P): A four-step process and period of time you should date before cohabitating.

Pussydos: The myriad cunt-styles you see in the lesbian community. (They include V formation, Mrs. Bigglesworth, cunnilingo incognito, soul patch, stripper stripe, vaginalina, the landing strip.)

Queersight: Similar to hindsight, but it's instead an acute sense of seeing how gay you were before you realized you liked pussy and came out of the closet.

Shooter: Dykes who try to knock off other women for their benefit, most common with good friends who secretly have feelings.

Swami: Lipstick's brother.

Tarnished star: A dyke who's slept with a dude.

Texas: Lipstick's wife, who is a fourth-generation Texan (a.k.a. Texas Two-Step, Texas Rose, Texas Lonestar, Little Texas, Téjas, Texas Longhorn).

The line: The very thin gray line that separates friendship and sexual relationship in the lesbian world.

Tiger: Dipstick's wife (a.k.a. The Incredible Girl at the End of my Rainbow).

Vaginal voodoo: What's left over on sex toys that were used with previous partners.

Virtual hoochy poos: Women you meet and have sex with online.

Yeouch-icardia: A serious disorder that makes your pussy hurt like a motherfucker during penetration or upon genital stimulation (a.k.a. dyspareunia).